Accounting for Truckers

Steven M. Bragg

AccountingTools®

ISBN 978-1-64221-148-1

Table of Contents

About the Author

Steven Bragg, CPA, has been the chief financial officer or controller of four companies, as well as a consulting manager at Ernst & Young. He received a master's degree in finance from Bentley College, an MBA from Babson College, and a Bachelor's degree in Economics from the University of Maine. He has been a two-time president of the Colorado Mountain Club, and is an avid alpine skier, mountain biker, and certified master diver. Mr. Bragg resides in Centennial, Colorado. He has written more than 300 books and courses, including *New Controller Guidebook*, *GAAP Guidebook*, and *Payroll Management*.

Steven maintains the accountingtools.com web site, which contains continuing professional education courses, the Accounting Best Practices podcast, and thousands of articles on accounting subjects.

Chapter 1
General Principles

Introduction

The trucking business can involve low margins, so it is essential to keep close watch over every business transaction, to ensure that you can generate a decent profit over time. Otherwise, poor accounting can lead to a rapid turn in the wrong direction, and possibly bankruptcy. In this book, we cover the accounting for truckers – including how to organize the business, set up a recordkeeping system, deal with the more common accounting transactions, and monitor costs.

In this chapter, we cover the general principles of accounting, including how an accounting system works and the information you will see on a trucking operation's financial statements.

Financial Accounting Basics

This introductory section is intended to give an overview of financial accounting basics. Its orientation is toward recording financial information about a business.

First, what do we mean by "financial" accounting? This refers to the recordation of information about money. Thus, we will talk about issuing an invoice to someone, as well as their payment of that invoice, but we will not address any change in the value of a company's overall business, since the latter situation does not involve a specific transaction involving money.

A *transaction* is a business event that has a monetary impact, such as selling transportation services to a customer or buying fuel from a vendor. In financial accounting, a transaction triggers the recording of information about the money involved in the event. For example, we would record in the accounting records such events (transactions) as:

- Incurring debt from a lender
- Paying a per diem stipend to an employee
- Selling trucking services to a customer
- Paying licensing fees to the government
- Paying wages to employees

We record this information in *accounts*. An account is a separate, detailed record about a specific item, such as expenditures for office supplies, or accounts receivable, or accounts payable. There can be many accounts, of which the most common are:

- *Cash*. This is the current balance of cash held by a business, usually in checking or savings accounts.
- *Accounts receivable*. These are sales on credit, which customers must pay for at a later date.

- *Fixed assets*. These are more expensive assets that the business plans to use for multiple years, such as trucks.
- *Accounts payable*. These are liabilities payable to suppliers that have not yet been paid.
- *Accrued expenses*. These are liabilities for which the business has not yet been billed, but for which it will eventually have to pay.
- *Debt*. This is cash loaned to the business by another party.
- *Equity*. This is the ownership interest in a business, which is the founding capital and any subsequent profits that have been retained in the business.
- *Revenue*. This is sales made to customers (both on credit and in cash).
- *Operating expenses*. This is the variety of expenses incurred to directly support trucking operations, such as fuel, equipment maintenance costs, and truck depreciation.
- *Administrative expenses*. These are a variety of expenses required to run a business, such as salaries, rent, utilities, and office supplies.
- *Income taxes*. These are the taxes paid to the government on any income earned by the business.

How do we enter information about transactions into these accounts? There are two ways to do so:

- *Software module entries*. If accounting software is being used to record financial accounting transactions, there will probably be on-line forms to fill out for each of the major transactions, such as creating a customer, or an invoice, or recording a supplier invoice. Every time one of these forms is filled out, the software automatically populates the accounts for the user.
- *Journal entries*. A journal entry form can be accessed in the accounting software. Alternatively, journal entries can be created by hand; this is a more customized way to record accounting information.

The accounts are stored in the *general ledger*. This is the master set of all accounts, in which are stored all of the business transactions that have been entered into the accounts with journal entries or software module entries. There may be subsidiary ledgers in which are stored high-volume transactions, such as sales or purchases. Thus, the general ledger is the go-to document for all of the detailed financial accounting information about a business.

To understand the detail for a particular account, such as the current amount of accounts receivable outstanding, access the general ledger for this information. In addition, most accounting software packages provide a number of reports that give better insights into the business than just reading through the accounts. In particular, there are aged accounts receivable and aged accounts payable reports that are useful for determining the current list of uncollected accounts receivable and unpaid accounts payable, respectively.

The general ledger is also the source document for the financial statements. There are several financial statements, which are:

- *Balance sheet*. This report lists the assets, liabilities, and equity of the business as of the report date.
- *Income statement*. This report lists the revenues, expenses, and profit or loss of the business for a specific period of time.
- *Statement of cash flows*. This report lists the cash inflows and outflows generated by the business for a specific period of time.

In summary, we have shown that financial accounting involves the recording of business transactions in accounts, which in turn are summarized in the general ledger, which in turn is used to create financial statements. We will now walk through the building blocks of an accounting system, starting with the accounting frameworks from which accounting rules are derived.

The Accounting Cycle

The *accounting cycle* is a sequential set of activities used to identify and record an entity's individual transactions. These transactions are then aggregated at the end of each reporting period into financial statements. The accounting cycle is essentially the core recordation activity that a bookkeeper engages in, and is the basis upon which the financial statements are constructed. The following discussion breaks the accounting cycle into the treatment of individual transactions and then closing the books at the end of the accounting period. The accounting cycle for individual transactions is:

1. Identify the event causing an accounting transaction, such as buying supplies, paying wages to employees, or selling trucking services to customers.
2. Prepare the business document associated with the accounting transaction, such as a supplier invoice, customer invoice, or cash receipt.
3. Identify which accounts are affected by the business document.
4. Record in the appropriate accounts in the accounting database the amounts noted on the business document.

The preceding accounting cycle steps were associated with individual transactions. The following accounting cycle steps are only used at the end of the reporting period, and are associated with the aggregate amounts of the preceding transactions:

5. Prepare a preliminary trial balance, which itemizes the debit and credit totals for each account.
6. Add accrued items, record estimated reserves, and correct errors in the preliminary trial balance with adjusting entries. Examples are the recordation of an expense for supplier invoices that have not yet arrived, and accruing for unpaid wages earned.
7. Prepare an adjusted trial balance, which incorporates the preliminary trial balance and all adjusting entries. It may require several iterations before this report accurately reflects the results of operations of the business.
8. Prepare financial statements from the adjusted trial balance.
9. Close the books for the reporting period.

In the following sections, we expand upon a number of the concepts just noted in the accounting cycle, including accounting transactions and journal entries.

Accounting Transactions

An *accounting transaction* is a business event having a monetary impact on the financial statements of a business. It is recorded in the accounting records of the organization. Examples of accounting transactions are:

- Sale in cash to a customer
- Sale on credit to a customer
- Receive cash in payment of an invoice owed by a customer
- Purchase fixed assets from a supplier
- Record the depreciation of a fixed asset over time
- Purchase consumable supplies from a supplier
- Investment in another business
- Borrow funds from a lender
- Sale of truck assets to a third party

Source Documents

Source documents are the physical basis upon which business transactions are recorded. They usually contain the following information:

- A description of the transaction
- The date of the transaction
- A specific amount of money
- An authorizing signature (in some cases)

Examples of source documents and their related business transactions that appear in the financial records are:

- *Bank statement.* This contains a number of adjustments to a company's book balance of cash on hand that the company should reference to bring its records into alignment with those of a bank.
- *Credit card receipt.* This can be used as evidence for a disbursement of funds from petty cash.
- *Receipt.* This document is used as evidence that goods have been purchased.
- *Supplier invoice.* This document supports the issuance of a cash, check, or electronic payment to a supplier. A supplier invoice also supports the recordation of an expense or fixed asset.
- *Time sheet.* This supports the issuance of a paycheck or electronic payment to an employee.

Double Entry Accounting

Double entry accounting is a record keeping system under which every transaction is recorded in at least two accounts. There is no upper limit on the number of accounts used in a transaction, but the minimum is two accounts. There are two columns in each account, with debit entries on the left and credit entries on the right. In double entry accounting, the total of all debit entries must match the total of all credit entries. When this happens, a transaction is said to be *in balance*. If the totals do not agree, the transaction is *out of balance*. An out of balance transaction must be corrected before financial statements can be created.

The definitions of a debit and credit are:

- A debit is an accounting entry that either increases an asset or expense account, or decreases a liability or equity account. It is positioned to the left in an accounting entry.
- A credit is an accounting entry that either increases a liability or equity account, or decreases an asset or expense account. It is positioned to the right in an accounting entry.

An account is a separate, detailed record associated with a specific asset, liability, equity, revenue, expense, gain, or loss. Examples of accounts are noted in the following table.

Characteristics of Sample Accounts

Account Name	Account Type	Normal Account Balance
Cash	Asset	Debit
Accounts receivable	Asset	Debit
Fixed assets	Asset	Debit
Accounts payable	Liability	Credit
Accrued liabilities	Liability	Credit
Notes payable	Liability	Credit
Common stock	Equity	Credit
Retained earnings	Equity	Credit
Revenue	Revenue	Credit
Cost of trucking services	Expense	Debit
Compensation expense	Expense	Debit
Utilities expense	Expense	Debit
Travel and entertainment	Expense	Debit
Gain on sale of asset	Gain	Credit
Loss on sale of asset	Loss	Debit

The key point with double entry accounting is that a single transaction always triggers a recordation in *at least* two accounts, as assets and liabilities gradually flow through a business and are converted into revenues, expenses, gains, and losses. We expand upon this concept in the next section.

The Accounting Equation

The *accounting equation* is the basis upon which the double entry accounting system is constructed. In essence, the accounting equation is:

$$Assets = Liabilities + Shareholders' Equity$$

The assets in the accounting equation are the resources that a company has available for its use, such as cash, accounts receivable, and fixed assets. The company pays for these resources by either incurring liabilities (which is the Liabilities part of the accounting equation) or by obtaining funding from investors (which is the Shareholders' Equity part of the equation). Thus, there are resources with offsetting claims against those resources, either from creditors or investors.

The Liabilities part of the equation is usually comprised of accounts payable that are owed to suppliers, a variety of accrued liabilities, such as income taxes, and debt payable to lenders.

The Shareholders' Equity part of the equation is more complex than simply being the amount paid to the company by investors. It is actually their initial investment, plus any subsequent gains, minus any subsequent losses, minus any dividends or other withdrawals paid to the investors.

This relationship between assets, liabilities, and shareholders' equity appears in the balance sheet, where the total of all assets always equals the sum of the liabilities and shareholders' equity sections.

The reason why the accounting equation is so important is that it is always true - and it forms the basis for all accounting transactions. At a general level, this means that whenever there is a recordable transaction, the choices for recording it all involve keeping the accounting equation in balance.

EXAMPLE

Creekside Trucking engages in the following series of transactions:

1. Creekside sells shares to an investor for $100,000. This increases the cash (asset) account as well as the capital (equity) account.
2. Creekside buys a $140,000 truck from a local distributor. This increases the fixed asset (asset) account as well as the payables (liability) account.
3. Creekside sells transport services to a customer for $1,500. This increases the revenue (sales) account and creates a billing to the customer, which increases the accounts receivable (asset) account.
4. Creekside collects cash from the customer to which it provided services. This increases the cash (asset) account by $1,500 and decreases the receivables (asset) account by $1,500.

6

These transactions appear in the following table.

Item	(Asset) Cash	(Asset) Receivables	(Asset) Fixed Asset		(Liability) Payables	(Equity) Capital	(Equity) Income
(1)	$100,000			=		$100,000	
(2)			$140,000	=	$140,000		
(3)		$1,500		=			$1,500
(4)	1,500	-$1,500		=			
Totals	$101,500	$0	$140,000	=	$140,000	$100,000	$1,500

In the example, note how every transaction is balanced within the accounting equation - either because there are changes on both sides of the equation, or because a transaction cancels itself out on one side of the equation (as was the case when the receivable was converted to cash).

The following exhibit shows how a number of typical accounting transactions are recorded within the framework of the accounting equation.

Impact of Transactions on Accounting Equation

Transaction Type	Assets	Liabilities + Equity
Buy fixed assets on credit	Fixed assets increase	Accounts payable (liability) increases
Pay rent	Cash decreases	Income (equity) decreases
Pay supplier invoices	Cash decreases	Accounts payable (liability) decreases
Sell services on credit	Accounts receivable increases	Income (equity) increases
Sell stock	Cash increases	Equity increases

Here are examples of each of the preceding transactions, where we show how they comply with the accounting equation:

- *Buy fixed assets on credit.* Creekside buys maintenance equipment on credit for $10,000. This increases the fixed assets (asset) account and increases the accounts payable (liability) account. Thus, the asset and liability sides of the transaction are equal.
- *Pay rent.* Creekside pays $4,000 in rent. This reduces the cash (asset) account and reduces the accounts payable (liabilities) account. Thus, the asset and liability sides of the transaction are equal.
- *Pay supplier invoices.* Creekside pays $29,000 on existing supplier invoices. This reduces the cash (asset) account by $29,000 and reduces the accounts payable (liability) account. Thus, the asset and liability sides of the transaction are equal.
- *Sell services on credit.* Creekside sell goods for $55,000 on credit. This increases the accounts receivable (asset) account by $55,000, and increases the revenue (equity) account. Thus, the asset and equity sides of the transaction are equal.

- *Sell stock.* Creekside sells $120,000 of its shares to investors. This increases the cash account (asset) by $120,000, and increases the capital stock (equity) account. Thus, the asset and equity sides of the transaction are equal.

Journal Entries

A *journal entry* is a formalized method for recording a business transaction. It is recorded in the accounting records of a business, usually in the general ledger, but sometimes in a subsidiary ledger that is then summarized and rolled forward into the general ledger.

Journal entries are used in a double entry accounting system, where the intent is to record every business transaction in at least two places. For example, when a company sells transport services to be paid later, this increases both the revenue account and the accounts receivable account.

The structure of a journal entry is:

- A header line may include a journal entry number and entry date.
- The first column includes the account number and account name into which the entry is recorded. This field is indented if it is for the account being credited.
- The second column contains the debit amount to be entered.
- The third column contains the credit amount to be entered.
- A footer line may also include a brief description of the reason for the entry.

Thus, the basic journal entry format is:

	Debit	Credit
Account name / number	$xx,xxx	
Account name / number		$xx,xxx

The structural rules of a journal entry are that there must be a minimum of two line items in the entry, and that the total amount entered in the debit column equals the total amount entered in the credit column.

A journal entry is usually printed and stored in a binder of accounting transactions, with backup materials attached that justify the entry. This information may be accessed by the company's auditors as part of their annual audit activities.

There are several types of journal entries, including:

- *Adjusting entry.* An adjusting entry is used at month-end to alter the financial statements to bring them into compliance with the relevant accounting framework. For example, a company could accrue unpaid wages at month-end in order to recognize the wages expense in the current period.

- *Compound entry.* This is a journal entry that includes more than two lines of entries. It is frequently used to record complex transactions, or several transactions at once. For example, the journal entry to record a payroll usually contains many lines, since it involves the recordation of numerous tax liabilities and payroll deductions.
- *Reversing entry.* This is an adjusting entry that is reversed as of the beginning of the following period, usually because an expense was accrued in the preceding period, and is no longer needed. Thus, a wage accrual in the preceding period is reversed in the next period, to be replaced by an actual payroll expenditure.

In general, journal entries are not used to record high-volume transactions, such as customer billings or supplier invoices. These transactions are handled through specialized software modules that present a standard on-line form to be filled out. Once the form is complete, the software automatically creates the accounting record.

Major Journal Entries

The following journal entry examples are intended to provide an outline of the general structure of the more common entries encountered. It is impossible to provide a complete set of journal entries that address every variation on every situation, since there are thousands of possible entries.

In each of the following journal entries, we state the topic, the relevant debit and credit, and additional comments as needed.

Revenue entries:

- *Sales entry.* Debit accounts receivable and credit sales. If a sale is for cash, the debit is to the cash account instead of the accounts receivable account.
- *Allowance for doubtful accounts entry.* Debit bad debt expense and credit the allowance for doubtful accounts. When actual bad debts are identified, debit the allowance account and credit the accounts receivable account, thereby clearing out the associated invoice.

Expense entries:

- *Accounts payable entry.* Debit the asset or expense account to which a purchase relates and credit the accounts payable account. When an account payable is paid, debit accounts payable and credit the cash account.
- *Payroll entry.* Debit the wages expense and payroll tax expense accounts, and credit the cash account. There may be additional credits to account for deductions from benefit expense accounts, if employees have permitted deductions for benefits to be taken from their pay.
- *Accrued expense entry.* Debit the applicable expense and credit the accrued expenses liability account. This entry is usually reversed automatically in the following period.

- *Depreciation entry*. Debit depreciation expense and credit accumulated depreciation. These accounts may be categorized by type of fixed asset.

Asset entries:

- *Cash reconciliation entry*. This entry can take many forms, but there is usually a debit to the bank fees account to recognize changes made by the bank, with a credit to the cash account. There may also be a debit to office supplies expense for any check supplies purchased and paid for through the bank account.
- *Prepaid expense adjustment entry*. When recognizing prepaid expenses as expenses, debit the applicable expense account and credit the prepaid expense asset account.
- *Fixed asset addition entry*. Debit the applicable fixed asset account and credit accounts payable.
- *Fixed asset derecognition entry*. Debit accumulated depreciation and credit the applicable fixed asset account. There may also be a gain or loss on the asset derecognition.

Liability entries:

See the preceding accounts payable and accrued expense entries.

Equity entries:

- *Dividend declaration*. Debit the retained earnings account and credit the dividends payable account. Once dividends are paid, this is a debit to the dividends payable account and a credit to the cash account. [note: only applies to a corporation]
- *Stock sale*. Debit the cash account and credit the common stock account.

These journal entry examples are only intended to provide an overview of the general types and formats of accounting entries. There are many variations on the entries presented here that are used to deal with a broad range of business transactions. More detailed journal entries are provided in the following chapter.

Depreciation

A particular concern for a trucking business is *depreciation*, which is the planned, gradual reduction in the recorded value of an asset over its useful life by charging it to expense. Depreciation is applied to fixed assets (which primarily means trucks, in the case of a trucking firm). The intent behind depreciation is to spread expense recognition over the period of time when a business expects to earn revenue from the use of an asset. The amount charged to expense does not include the estimated salvage value of the asset at the end of its useful life.

EXAMPLE

Surfside Trucking acquires a semi-truck for $120,000, and plans to operate it for the next ten years. The owner expects that he will be able to sell off the vehicle at the end of ten years for $20,000. Under the straight-line method of depreciation, this would require the firm to charge $10,000 to depreciation expense in each of the next ten years, so that the book value of the semi-truck will be $20,000 ten years from now.

There are also accelerated depreciation methods that can be used instead of the straight-line method, which can be useful for recognizing more depreciation expense during the early years of an asset's usage period.

The Accruals Concept

An *accrual* is a journal entry that is used to recognize revenues and expenses that have been earned or consumed, respectively, and for which the related source documents have not yet been received or generated. Accruals are needed to ensure that all revenue and expense elements are recognized within the correct reporting period, irrespective of the timing of related cash flows. Without accruals, the amount of revenue, expense, and profit or loss in a period will not necessarily reflect the actual level of economic activity within a business. Accruals are a key part of the closing process used to create financial statements under the accrual basis of accounting; without accruals, financial statements would be considerably less accurate.

It is most efficient to initially record most accruals as reversing entries. This is a useful feature when a business is expecting to issue an invoice to a customer or receive an invoice from a supplier in the following period. For example, a bookkeeper may know that a supplier invoice for $20,000 will arrive a few days after the end of a month, but she wants to close the books as soon as possible. Accordingly, she records a $20,000 reversing entry to recognize the expense in the current month. In the next month, the accrual reverses, creating a negative $20,000 expense that is offset by the arrival and recordation of the supplier invoice.

Examples of accruals that a business might record are:

- *Expense accrual for interest.* A local lender issues a loan to a business, and sends the borrower an invoice each month, detailing the amount of interest owed. The borrower can record the interest expense in advance of invoice receipt by recording accrued interest.
- *Expense accrual for wages.* An employer pays its employees once a month for the hours they have worked through the 26th day of the month. The employer can accrue all additional wages earned from the 27th through the last day of the month, to ensure that the full amount of the wage expense is recognized.
- *Sales accrual.* A trucking firm is transporting goods for the federal government, which it will bill when the work has been completed. In the meantime,

the company can accrue revenue for the amount of work completed to date, even though the work has not yet been billed.

If a business records its transactions under the cash basis of accounting, it does not use accruals. Instead, the organization records transactions only when it either pays out or receives cash. See the later Cash Basis of Accounting section for an explanation of this concept.

The Realization Concept

The *realization principle* is the concept that revenue can only be recognized once the underlying goods or services associated with the revenue have been delivered or rendered, respectively. Thus, revenue can only be recognized after it has been earned. The best way to understand the realization concept is through an example. A customer pays $1,000 in advance for the delivery of goods. The trucking firm does not realize the $1,000 of revenue until the delivery has been completed. Consequently, the $1,000 is initially recorded as a liability, which is then shifted to revenue only after the shipment has been completed.

The realization concept is most often violated when a company wants to accelerate the recognition of revenue, and so books revenues in advance of all related earning activities being completed.

Accrual Basis of Accounting

The *accrual basis of accounting* is the concept of recording revenues when earned and expenses as incurred. This concept differs from the cash basis of accounting, under which revenues are recorded when cash is received, and expenses are recorded when cash is paid. For example, a company operating under the accrual basis of accounting will record a sale as soon as it issues an invoice to a customer, while a cash basis company would instead wait to be paid before it records the sale. Similarly, an accrual basis company will record an expense as incurred, while a cash basis company would instead wait to pay its supplier before recording the expense.

The accrual basis tends to provide more even recognition of revenues and expenses over time than the cash basis, and so is considered to be the most valid accounting system for ascertaining the results of operations, financial position, and cash flows of a business. In particular, it supports the matching principle, under which revenues and all related expenses are to be recorded within the same reporting period; by doing so, it should be possible to see the full extent of the profits and losses associated with specific business transactions within a single reporting period.

EXAMPLE

Harry completes a long-haul transport job in February, for which he invoices the customer $5,000, to be paid in 30 days. He also incurs $2,000 of fuel costs on the company debit card, for which payment is immediately extracted from the company's bank account. Under the accrual basis of accounting, both the revenue and expense would appear in the February income statement, so that Harry can see the full impact of the job. However, under the cash basis of accounting, he would only see the fuel cost appearing as an expense in February, with the customer billing appearing a month or two later, when the customer pays the bill.

The accrual basis requires the use of estimated reserves in certain areas. For example, a company should recognize an expense for estimated bad debts that have not yet been incurred. By doing so, all expenses related to a revenue transaction are recorded at the same time as the revenue, which results in an income statement that fully reflects the results of operations. These estimates may not be entirely accurate, and so can lead to materially inaccurate financial statements. Consequently, care must be used when estimating reserves.

Cash Basis of Accounting

The *cash basis of accounting* is the practice of only recording revenue when cash is received from a customer, and recording expenses only when cash has been paid out. The cash basis is commonly used by individuals and small businesses, especially those with no inventory. A trucking company will frequently begin keeping its books under the cash basis, and then switch to the accrual basis of accounting (see the preceding section) when it has grown to a sufficient size. The cash basis of accounting has the following advantages:

- *Taxation.* The method is commonly used to record financial results for tax purposes, since a business can accelerate some payments in order to reduce its taxable profits, thereby deferring its tax liability.
- *Ease of use.* A person requires a reduced knowledge of accounting to keep records under the cash basis.

However, the cash basis of accounting also suffers from the following problems:

- *Accuracy.* The cash basis yields less accurate results than the accrual basis of accounting, since the timing of cash flows does not necessarily reflect the proper timing of changes in the financial condition of a business. For example, if a contract with a customer does not allow a business to issue an invoice until the end of a job, the company will be unable to report any revenue until the invoice has been issued and cash received.
- *Manipulation.* A business can alter its reported results by not cashing received checks or altering the payment timing for its liabilities.

- *Lending.* Lenders do not feel that the cash basis generates overly accurate financial statements, and so may refuse to lend money to a business reporting under the cash basis.
- *Audited financial statements.* Auditors will not approve financial statements that were compiled under the cash basis, so a company will need to convert to the accrual basis if it wants to have audited financial statements.
- *Management reporting.* Since the results of cash basis financial statements can be inaccurate, management reports should not be issued that are based upon it.

In short, the numerous problems with the cash basis of accounting usually cause businesses to abandon it after they move beyond their initial startup phases.

The Financial Statements

There are three financial statements, which are the income statement, balance sheet, and statement of cash flows. Of the three, the income statement is the simplest to compile, and is likely to give you the most immediately useful information about how well the business is doing.

The Income Statement

The income statement contains the results of a firm's operations during a reporting period, showing revenues and expenses, and the resulting profit or loss. You can structure the income statement for your business in any way you want, but it is typically laid out with revenues at the top, followed by those expenses you are most interested in monitoring. For a trucking operation, these expenses are likely to include compensation, payroll taxes, benefits, fuel, and maintenance. An example of how this layout might look appears in the following exhibit.

Income Statement
Jones Trucking
For the Quarter Ended March 31, 20X1

Revenue	$xxx
Expenses	
Compensation expense	$xxx
Payroll taxes expense	xxx
Employee benefits expense	xxx
Fuel expense	xxx
Maintenance expense	xxx
Insurance expense	xxx
Depreciation expense	xxx
Utilities expense	xxx
Licensing expense	xxx
Other expenses	xxx
Total expenses	$xxx
Profit before tax	$xxx

In the preceding income statement format, expenses are clustered by compensation, then truck expenses, and then all other expenses. You might also consider a format in which the line items are listed alphabetically, or in descending order by dollar amounts. In short, pick whichever format is most informational for you.

> **Tip:** In a larger trucking firm, you might want to aggregate expenses by department, so that only the totals are shown on the report for each department. Possible departments might be accounting, corporate, human resources, maintenance, logistics, and dispatch.

The Balance Sheet

A balance sheet presents information about an entity's assets, liabilities, and shareholders' equity, where the compiled result must match the accounting equation, as noted earlier in this chapter. The balance sheet reports the aggregate effect of transactions as of a specific date. It is used to assess your organization's liquidity and ability to pay its debts. It provides an at-a-glance indicator of the overall financial situation of a business.

There is no specific requirement for the line items to be included in the balance sheet. The following line items, at a minimum, are normally included in it:

Current Assets:

- Cash
- Accounts receivable
- Investments

Non-Current Assets:

- Fixed assets
- Other assets

Current Liabilities:

- Accounts payable
- Accrued expenses
- Current tax liabilities
- Current portion of loans payable
- Other liabilities

Non-Current Liabilities:

- Loans payable
- Deferred tax liabilities
- Other non-current liabilities

Equity:

- Capital stock
- Retained earnings

The following exhibit shows a balance sheet which presents information as of the end of two fiscal years.

Road Haulers, LLC
Balance Sheet
As of December 31, 20X2 and 20X1

(000s)	12/31/20X2	12/31/20X1
ASSETS		
Current assets		
Cash	$270,000	$215,000
Accounts receivable	286,000	267,000
Other current assets	15,000	27,000
Total current assets	$571,000	$509,000
Non-current assets		
Fixed assets	776,000	754,000
Total assets	$1,347,000	$1,263,000
LIABILITIES AND EQUITY		
Current liabilities		
Accounts payable	$217,000	$198,000
Short-term borrowings	133,000	202,000
Current portion of long-term borrowings	5,000	5,000
Current tax payable	26,000	23,000
Accrued expenses	9,000	13,000
Total current liabilities	$390,000	$441,000
Non-current liabilities		
Long-term debt	85,000	65,000
Deferred taxes	19,000	17,000
Total non-current liabilities	$104,000	$82,000
Total liabilities	$494,000	$523,000
Shareholders' equity		
Capital	115,000	115,000
Retained earnings	738,000	625,000
Total equity	$853,000	$740,000
Total liabilities and equity	$1,347,000	$1,263,000

An asset on the balance sheet should be classified as current when you expect to sell or consume it within 12 months after the reporting period. Classify all other assets as non-current.

Classify all of the following as current assets:

- *Cash.* This is cash available for current operations, as well as any short-term, highly liquid investments that are readily convertible to known amounts of cash and which are so near their maturities that they present an insignificant risk of value changes. Do not include cash whose withdrawal is restricted, to be used for other than current operations, or segregated for the liquidation of long-term debts; such items should be classified as longer-term.
- *Accounts receivable.* This includes trade accounts, notes, and acceptances that are receivable. Also, include receivables from officers, employees, and others if they are collectible within a year. Do not include any receivable that will not be collected within 12 months; such items should be classified as longer-term.
- *Marketable securities.* This includes those securities representing the investment of cash available for current operations.
- *Prepaid expenses.* This includes prepayments for insurance, interest, rent, taxes, advertising services, and operating supplies.

A liability is classified as current when you expect to settle it within 12 months after the reporting period. Classify all other liabilities as non-current.

Classify all of the following as current liabilities:

- *Payables.* This is all accounts payable incurred in the acquisition of goods, services, and administrative expenditures to support operations.
- *Accruals.* This is accrued expenses for items directly related to operations, such as accruals for compensation, rentals, and various taxes.
- *Short-term debts.* This is debts maturing within the next 12 months.

Current liabilities include accruals for amounts that can only be determined approximately, such as bonuses.

The Statement of Cash Flows

It is essential to fully understand how much cash is coming in and how much is going out. If an imbalance arises where inbound cash flows unexpectedly fall off, the business might not be able to pay its creditors. To guard against this, a useful tool is the statement of cash flows, which itemizes where cash is coming from and how it is being used.

The statement of cash flows contains information about the flows of cash into and out of a company; in particular, it shows the extent of those company activities that generate and use cash. The primary activities are:

- *Operating activities*. These are an entity's primary revenue-producing activities. Examples of operating activities are cash receipts from the sale of trucking services, as well as from amounts received or paid to settle lawsuits, fines, payments to employees and suppliers, cash payments to lenders for interest, and contributions to charity.
- *Investing activities*. These involve the acquisition and disposal of long-term assets. Examples of investing activities are cash receipts from the sale of property, the sale of the debt or equity instruments of other entities, the repayment of loans made to other entities, and proceeds from insurance settlements related to damaged assets. Examples of cash payments that are investment activities include the acquisition of trucks, as well as the purchase of the debt or equity of other entities.
- *Financing activities*. These are the activities resulting in alterations to the amount of contributed equity and the entity's borrowings. Examples of financing activities include cash receipts from the sale of the entity's own equity instruments or from issuing debt, and cash payments to buy back shares, pay dividends, and pay off outstanding debt.

The statement of cash flows also incorporates the concept of cash and cash equivalents. A *cash equivalent* is a short-term, very liquid investment that is easily convertible into a known amount of cash, and which is so near its maturity that it presents an insignificant risk of a change in value because of changes in interest rates.

In a statement of cash flows, the presentation begins with net income or loss, with subsequent additions to or deductions from that amount for non-cash revenue and expense items, resulting in net income provided by operating activities. The format of the report appears in the following exhibit.

Lowry Trucking
Statement of Cash Flows
For the year ended 12/31/20X1

Cash flows from operating activities		
Net income		$100,000
Adjustments for:		
Depreciation and amortization	$125,000	
Provision for losses on accounts receivable	20,000	
Gain on sale of facility	-65,000	
		80,000
Increase in trade receivables	-25,000	
Increase in trade payables	50,000	
		25,000
Cash generated from operations		205,000
Cash flows from investing activities		
Purchase of fixed assets	-200,000	
Proceeds from sale of equipment	35,000	
Net cash used in investing activities		-165,000
Cash flows from financing activities		
Proceeds from sale of ownership interest	150,000	
Proceeds from issuance of long-term debt	75,000	
Net cash used in financing activities		225,000
Net increase in cash and cash equivalents		265,000
Cash and cash equivalents at beginning of period		100,000
Cash and cash equivalents at end of period		$365,000

A statement of cash flows does not necessarily match the profit and loss information presented on your income statement. It is quite possible that the income statement will show a profit, while the statement of cash flows reveals that your cash flows are solidly negative. There can be multiple reasons for this, such as a large investment in a truck that has absorbed your excess cash, or perhaps a number of unpaid customer bills. To guard against this, do not just rely on the income statement. Instead, create a statement of cash flows at the same time, and review it in detail to discern how the company's cash is being used.

Summary

The main focus of this chapter was to reveal how business transactions are recorded in the accounting system. The level of detail given was intended to provide you with a basic understanding of the process, rather than the more detailed knowledge needed to actually operate such a system. We then went on to describe the financial statements, which are your main source of information about how your trucking business is performing. These reports should be produced automatically by your accounting software, making them quite easy to access. In the next chapter, we describe a series of journal entries that the bookkeeper for a trucking operation is most likely to use.

Chapter 2
Accounting Transactions for Trucking

Introduction

This chapter contains the accounting transactions that a trucking firm is very likely to use, including Department of Transportation fees, depreciation, permit fees, per diem expenditures, payroll, and more.

Driving School Expenditures

As an inducement to join, a trucking firm may offer to pay the driving school fees for new drivers, in exchange for them promising to remain with the firm for a minimum period of time, such as a year. It may be possible to initially account for this expenditure as an asset and charge it to expense over the time period to which a driver has committed to work for the firm. If so, the journal entry is to initially record the driving school fee as an asset, and charge a portion of this cost to expense over the commitment period. An example appears next, where we are initially recording a $6,000 school expenditure as an asset, followed by a monthly entry to charge it to expense over a one-year commitment period.

	Debit	Credit
Driving school fees [asset]	6,000	
Cash [asset]		6,000
To initially record driving school fees as an asset		

	Debit	Credit
Driving school expense [expense]	500	
Driving school fees [asset]		500
To record monthly charge to expense for driving school fees asset		

The problem with this approach is that drivers may leave the firm before their commitment period has been completed. If the business has no way of reliably recovering its expenses from these drivers, then it will be necessary to instead charge these expenditures straight to expense as soon as they are incurred. An example appears next.

	Debit	Credit
Driving school expense [expense]	6,000	
Cash [asset]		6,000
To record driving school fees charged to expense as incurred		

Department of Transportation Fees

Any trucking business will pay fees to the Department of Transportation (DOT) for each state in which it operates, such as an annual fee for each vehicle registered to the business. This fee is charged to expense as incurred, and may be recorded in a separate account for each state. Using a separate account for each state is recommended, since you can more easily scan the accounts to see if any payments have not been made to certain states; this is a good way to determine if a DOT billing might not have been issued, or not received. An example of this entry follows.

	Debit	Credit
DOT fees - Colorado [expense]	400	
Accounts payable [liability]		400
To record Department of Transportation registration fees		

Depreciation

A trucking firm that owns its trucks will have to charge their acquisition cost to depreciation over their useful lives. This requires the following journal entry, where depreciation expense is charged, along with an accumulated depreciation account. The accumulated depreciation account is classified as a contra account, because it is paired with and offsets the fixed assets account. The amount of accumulated depreciation reduces the net amount of fixed assets recorded on the balance sheet.

	Debit	Credit
Depreciation expense [expense]	5,000	
Accumulated depreciation [contra asset]		5,000
To record periodic depreciation expense		

When a fixed asset is retired, the balances in the fixed asset and accumulated depreciation accounts are reversed, which flushes both balances out of the accounting records, removing them from the balance sheet. A typical entry is noted below.

	Debit	Credit
Accumulated depreciation [contra asset]	100,000	
Fixed assets [asset]		100,000
To record the elimination of a fixed asset		

International Registration Plan Tags

An international registration plan tag is a license plate, which is issued by your state's DOT. This tag allows your trucks to operate across state lines. A registration fee must be paid to initially obtain these tags, as well as an annual renewal fee. This expense can be recorded in a separate account, as shown in the following example.

	Debit	Credit
IRP tag fees [expense]	400	
Accounts payable [liability]		400
To record international registration plan tag fees		

International Fuel Tax Agreement Payments

The International Fuel Tax Agreement (IFTA) is an arrangement among U.S. states and Canadian provinces, where commercial motor carriers are allowed to register in one state and have the related tax assessments be paid out to all participating areas according to their fair share of the miles driven and fuel used by those motor carriers. The IFTA was created for truckers who frequently cross state lines on their routes, and generally simplifies accounting and the payment of fuel taxes. Commercial trucking operations hold permits that dictate a specific tax rate on motor fuel, so that their payouts can be calculated and adjusted (money owned or credited) on a quarterly basis. The supporting documentation used for these payments includes the vehicle mileage record, distance records, fuel records, and tax-paid retail fuel purchase receipts. If you do not file a quarterly tax return by the due date or fail to pay the tax owed, the presiding state government will charge a penalty and interest. The typical accounting entry associated with this filing is shown below.

	Debit	Credit
IFTA fuel tax expense [expense]	2,000	
Accounts payable [liability]		2,000
To record IFTA quarterly fuel tax expense		

Heavy Highway Vehicle Use Tax

Any business that has registered a heavy highway motor vehicle with a taxable gross weight of 55,000 pounds or more at the time of first use on the public highways must file Form 2290, *Heavy Highway Vehicle Use Tax Return*. The proceeds from this tax are used to pay for highway infrastructure and road maintenance. The amount can be fairly substantial when the related use tax is paid for a larger truck fleet.

Consequently, it can make sense to track this expenditure in a separate account. In the following example, we show the initial recordation of the expense.

	Debit	Credit
Heavy highway vehicle use tax [expense]	1,200	
Accounts payable [liability]		1,200
To record heavy highway vehicle use tax		

Other Permit Fees

A variety of other permits may be required for your business, such as oversize and overweight vehicle permits. The fees associated with these other permits can be aggregated into a single account, as shown in the following example. However, if you want to track the expenses associated with a particular type of permit more closely, then just create an additional expense account for it, and store the related expenditures there.

	Debit	Credit
Other permit fees [expense]	200	
Accounts payable [liability]		200
To record other permit fees		

Payroll Journal Entry

The primary journal entry for payroll is the summary-level entry that is compiled from the payroll register, and which is recorded in either the payroll journal or the general ledger. This entry usually includes debits for the wages expense and the company's portion of payroll taxes. There will also be credits to a number of other accounts, each one detailing the liability for payroll taxes that have not been paid, as well as for the amount of cash already paid to employees for their net pay. The basic entry appears in the following exhibit.

	Debit	Credit
Wages expense [expense]	10,000	
Payroll taxes expense [expense]	910	
Cash [asset]		6,840
Federal withholding taxes payable [liability]		2,000
Social security taxes payable [liability]		1,240
Medicare taxes payable [liability]		580
Federal unemployment taxes payable [liability]		150
State unemployment taxes payable [liability]		25
Garnishments payable [liability]		75
To record periodic payroll transaction for the staff		

Per Diem Expenditures

When truckers are expected to drive significant distances, you might choose to pay them a per diem amount per day on the road, which is a stipend that is intended to cover their meals and lodging. A sample entry follows:

	Debit	Credit
Driver per diem payments [expense]	350	
Accounts payable [liability]		350
To record per diem stipends paid to drivers		

Sales Tax Remittances

Depending on the state in which your trucks conduct operations, it may be necessary to withhold sales tax on the invoices issued to your customers. Withheld sales taxes are classified as a liability, not an expense, since they are supposed to be remitted to the applicable state government. This means that there are two journal entries, one for the initial billing to the customer, and another for the sales tax remittance to the government. The two entries are shown below.

	Debit	Credit
Accounts receivable [asset]	1,040	
Sales [revenue]		1,000
Sales taxes payable [liability]		40
To record customer invoice with sales tax		

	Debit	Credit
Sales taxes payable [liability]	40	
Cash [asset]		40
To remit sales taxes to the government		

Summary

In this chapter, we have shown the general format used for a variety of trucking expenditures, while also noting whether each line item is an expense, liability, asset, and so forth. The intent is to provide a template for actual journal entries related to these types of transactions. In the following chapter, we provide details about one of the most common accounting areas for a trucking firm to deal with – payroll.

Chapter 3
Payroll Processing

Introduction

Payroll processing can be quite a pain for a trucking operation, because you may have to pay a large number of truckers, and all of them must have their compensation calculated, withholdings taken, and payroll taxes determined. Payroll taxes include social security, Medicare, and unemployment insurance, each of which has separate calculation rules.

Once you have completed these tasks, the related payroll taxes and withheld income taxes must be forwarded to the IRS through its Electronic Filing and Tax Payment System (EFTPS). Your state will likely also have a payroll tax remittance system. In this chapter, we cover the essentials of how to process payroll.

The Independent Contractor Designation

Perhaps the single most critical payroll issue for a trucking business is whether a driver should be classified as an independent contractor. The point is a major one, since the business can avoid a significant liability for deducting payroll taxes and withholding income taxes, as well as for avoiding the payment of matching amounts of social security and Medicare taxes.

To determine whether a person can be classified as an independent contractor, review the entire working relationship between the company and the person, and arrive at a decision based on the complete body of evidence. There are three categories of facts to consider, which are[1]:

- *Behavioral control.* A person is an employee if the business has the right to direct and control how the person does the task for which he was hired. The amount of control is based on the level of instruction regarding such issues as when and where to work, what equipment to use, which employees to use, where to buy supplies, what sequence of tasks to follow, and so forth. Behavioral control can include training by the company to perform services in a particular way.
- *Financial control.* Facts indicative of financial control by the company are the extent to which a worker is reimbursed for business expenses, the amount of investment by the worker in the business, the extent to which the worker sells his services to other parties, whether the amount paid to the person is based on time worked rather than for a work product, and whether the worker can participate in a profit or loss.

---

[1] As noted in IRS Publication 15-A, *Employer's Supplemental Tax Guide*, Employee or Independent Contractor?

- *Type of relationship.* A person is more likely to be considered an independent contractor if there is a written contract describing the relationship of the parties, the business does not provide benefits to the person, the relationship is not permanent, and the services performed are not a key aspect of the regular business of the company.

EXAMPLE

Gene Brooks is a truck driver. He does delivery jobs on behalf of Ultimate Trucking, but uses his own truck, routinely engages in transport jobs for other trucking firms, and sets his own hours. He is paid a fixed rate based on the completion of each job. Mr. Brooks is an independent contractor.

EXAMPLE

Alvin Simmons is a truck driver. He is based out of the headquarters of Fairmont Trucking. He is on call each day, and drives local routes as directed by the dispatching department, using the company's trucks. He is paid a standard hourly rate. Mr. Simmons is an employee.

The Payroll Cycle

One of the more important payroll management decisions is how long to set the payroll cycle. Each payroll requires a great deal of effort by the payroll staff to collect information about time worked, locate and correct errors, process wage rate and deduction changes, calculate pay, and issue payments. Consequently, it makes a great deal of sense to extend the duration of payroll cycles.

If payrolls are spaced at short intervals, such as weekly, the payroll staff has to prepare 52 payrolls per year. Conversely, paying employees once a month reduces the payroll staff's payroll preparation activities by approximately three-quarters. Since paying employees just once a month can be a burden on the employees, companies frequently adopt a half-way measure, paying employees either twice a month (the *semimonthly* payroll) or once every two weeks (the *biweekly* payroll). The semimonthly payroll cycle results in processing 24 payrolls per year, while the biweekly payroll cycle requires the processing of 26 payrolls per year.

An example of a weekly payroll cycle appears in the following exhibit, where employees are paid every Tuesday for the hours they worked in the preceding week.

Weekly Payroll Cycle

January						
S	M	T	W	T	F	S
	1	2	3	4	5	6
7	8	9	10	11	12	13
14	15	16	17	18	19	20
21	22	23	24	25	26	27
28	29	30	31			

An example of a biweekly payroll cycle appears in the following exhibit, where employees are paid every other Tuesday for the hours worked in the preceding two weeks.

Biweekly Payroll Cycle

January						
S	M	T	W	T	F	S
	1	2	3	4	5	6
7	8	9	10	11	12	13
14	15	16	17	18	19	20
21	22	23	24	25	26	27
28	29	30	31			

An example of a semimonthly payroll cycle appears in the following exhibit, where employees are paid on the 15th and last days of the month.

Semimonthly Payroll Cycle

January						
S	M	T	W	T	F	S
	1	2	3	4	5	6
7	8	9	10	11	12	13
14	15	16	17	18	19	20
21	22	23	24	25	26	27
28	29	30	31			

An argument in favor of the biweekly payroll is that employees become accustomed to receiving two paychecks per month, plus two "free" paychecks during the year, which has a somewhat more positive impact on employee morale. Nonetheless, the semimonthly payroll represents a slight improvement over the biweekly payroll from the perspective of payroll department efficiency, and is therefore recommended.

If employees are accustomed to a weekly payroll cycle and they are switched to one of a longer duration, expect to have some employees complain about not having enough cash to see them through the initial increased payroll cycle. This problem can be mitigated by extending pay advances to employees during the initial conversion to the longer payroll cycle. Once employees receive their larger paychecks under the new payroll cycle, they should be able to support themselves and will no longer need an advance.

> **Tip:** Avoid paying employees on a per-job basis. Doing so results in an excessively large number of payments, which is not a good use of staff time. Processing payroll on a regularly-scheduled basis is much more efficient.

Procedure: Add an Employee

Use the following procedure to add an employee to the payroll system:

1. Verify the employee's authorization to work in the United States, and complete the Form I-9, *Employment Eligibility Verification.*
2. Have the employee fill out a Form W-4, *Employee's Withholding Certificate.*
3. Verify the authorization signature on the employee offer sheet.
4. Create a record for the employee in the payroll system and enter the following information:

   - Employee name
   - Employee address
   - Employee social security number
   - Employee marriage status
   - Withholding amounts
   - Start date
   - Base wage or salary
   - Banking information (for direct deposit)

5. Create an employee folder, insert all related documents in it, and store it in a locked storage area.

Procedure: Timesheet Data Collection

If timesheets are used to collect information about hours worked, use the following procedure:

1. Issue a reminder to employees a few days in advance to make sure their timesheets are up-to-date.
2. Print a list of all employees who are supposed to submit timesheets.
3. Sort all timesheets received by employee last name.

4. Compare the timesheets to the employee list, and note which employees have not yet submitted their timesheets.
5. Compare the employee list to the schedule of employees who are on vacation, and cross off the names of those employees who did not submit timesheets and who are on vacation.
6. Review all timesheets for errors, such as missing beginning and ending times, and vacation used that has not been earned, and return them to employees for correction.
7. Forward all timesheets containing overtime hours to management for approval.
8. Verify that all time sheets returned for correction or approval have been returned.
9. Add up the time worked on each sheet and note the total hours worked at the top of the sheet.
10. Forward the approved and summarized time sheets to accounting for entry into the payroll processing system.

Procedure: Process Payroll

Use the following procedure to process payroll. In the procedure, we assume that in-house payroll software is being used, though data entry into an outsourced payroll processing system would be similar.

1. Update the employee master file with the following changes, if any:
   - Change of employee name
   - Change of employee address
   - Change of employee pay rate
   - Change of employee marriage status and/or withholding amount
   - Change of employee payment method
   - Change of employee status to inactive

2. Verify that the payroll module is set for the correct pay period.
3. Enter the amount of regular and overtime hours worked by each employee.
4. Verify that the hours of all wage-earning employees have been entered.
5. Enter the amounts of any manual paychecks that have not yet been recorded in the payroll system.
6. Manually calculate the amount payable to any employee who has left the company, including their unused vacation time and severance pay.
7. Enter any changes to the standard deductions from employee pay, including the following:
   - Cafeteria plan
   - Charitable contributions
   - Dental insurance
   - Disability insurance
   - Garnishments

- Life insurance
- Medical insurance
- Pension plans

8. Have the software process all pay calculations for the period.
9. Print the following reports and review the underlying transactions for errors. Process payroll again until these issues have been corrected.

  - Negative deductions report
  - Negative taxes report
  - Preliminary payroll register
  - Sorted list of wages paid

10. Issue payments to employees (see next procedure)
11. Issue payroll reports to management.
12. Back up the payroll database.
13. Lock down the payroll period in the payroll module for the period just completed, to prevent unauthorized changes.
14. Deposit payroll taxes and verify their transmission to the government.
15. Investigate all transaction errors encountered, and initiate changes to mitigate their continuing occurrence.

Procedure: Issue Payments to Employees

Use the following procedure to issue payments to employees. In the procedure, we assume the use of both paychecks and direct deposit.

1. Print the preliminary payroll register and review it for errors. Adjust transactions as necessary to correct errors, and re-process payroll as needed.
2. Review and initial the final version of this preliminary report.
3. Remove check stock from the locked storage cabinet.
4. Print paychecks for those employees receiving paychecks.
5. Review the paychecks and reprint them if necessary.
6. Accept the printed batch in the payroll software.
7. Print remittance advices for those employees receiving direct deposit payments.
8. Review the advices and reprint them if necessary.
9. Accept the printed batch in the payroll software.
10. Return any remaining unused checks to the locked storage area, and log the range of check numbers that were used.
11. Print the final payroll register.
12. Store the final payroll register in the payroll archives area.
13. Export the direct deposit payments file to the direct deposit processor, and verify receipt of the file by the processor. Correct any direct deposit failures that arise.
14. Have an authorized check signer sign all paychecks.
15. Stuff the checks and remittance advices into envelopes.

16. Deliver the paychecks and remittance advices to employees.
17. For off-site locations, send paychecks and remittance advices by overnight delivery service.

Payroll Register

We made several references to the *payroll register* earlier in this chapter. This is the primary internal report generated by the payroll system. It itemizes the calculation of wages, taxes, and deductions for each employee for each payroll. There are multiple uses for the payroll register, including:

- *Investigation*. It is the starting point for the investigation of many issues involving employee pay.
- *Journal entries*. Create journal entries to record a payroll based on the information in the register.
- *Payments*. If manual check payments are being created, the source document for these payments is the register.
- *Reports*. The information on almost any management report related to payroll is drawn from the register.

The format of the payroll register is built into the payroll software, and so will vary somewhat by payroll system. If payroll processing is outsourced, the supplier will issue its own version of the payroll register as part of its basic service package. The following exhibit contains a typical payroll register format, with overtime and state and local taxes removed in order to compress the presentation.

Sample Payroll Register

Empl. Nbr.	Employee Name	Hours Worked	Rate/ Hour	Gross Wages	Taxes	Other Deductions	Check Nbr.	Net Pay
100	Johnson, Mark	40	18.12	724.80	55.45	28.00	5403	641.35
105	Olds, Gary	27	36.25	978.75	74.87	42.25	5404	861.63
107	Zeff, Morton	40	24.00	960.00	73.44	83.00	5405	803.56
111	Quill, Davis	40	15.00	600.00	45.90	10.10	5406	544.00
116	Pincus, Joseph	35	27.75	971.25	74.30	37.50	5407	859.45

Payroll Outsourcing

When payroll is outsourced, this rarely means that the entire payroll function is physically transferred away from the company. Instead, only the payroll calculation, tax remittance, and employee payment functions are shifted to a third party. The employer is still responsible for collecting information about hours worked, as well as inputting information about employees.

The splitting of responsibilities between the employer and its payroll supplier are roughly as follows:

Employer responsibilities:

- Collect hours worked
- Collect employee allowance, deduction, and personal information
- Input the preceding information into the payroll system maintained by the supplier
- Distribute paychecks and remittance advices forwarded by the supplier
- Record payroll transactions based on reports issued by the supplier

Supplier responsibilities:

- Calculate wages based on hours worked
- Calculate tax deductions and withholdings
- Create paychecks, initiate direct deposit payments, and forward cash to payroll debit cards
- Remit taxes and withholdings to government entities
- Issue standard reports to clients
- Issue W-2 forms to employees following the end of the calendar year

The reason for this split is that payroll suppliers are focusing on the data processing aspects of payroll, where they use mainframe-based computers to handle the payroll processing for large numbers of clients. The fixed cost of these systems is high, but suppliers can achieve considerable profitability if they have many clients using their systems. What a payroll supplier wants to avoid is the low value-added and highly error-prone tasks of collecting information about employees and entering it into the payroll system. Thus, payroll suppliers are narrowly focused on the highest value-added portion of the tasks handled by the payroll department.

Reasons to Outsource Payroll

Payroll is one of the most commonly outsourced company functions. There are several good reasons for this, which are:

- *Backups*. Suppliers backup a company's payroll information continually, and should have off-site storage of the backups, as well.
- *Check stuffing*. All payroll suppliers will stuff paychecks into envelopes, which eliminates a low-end clerical task that the payroll staff would otherwise have to perform.
- *Direct deposit*. Most payroll suppliers have the capability to issue payments to employees by direct deposit. Companies that process their payroll in-house can also do this, but only through the services of a third party that handles direct deposit.

- *Expert staff.* Suppliers have a core of highly-trained staff who not only know their systems and payroll regulations quite well, but who also provide training to clients, as well as advice over the phone.
- *Multi-location processing.* Larger payroll suppliers have locations in most major cities, and so can directly deliver paychecks to most urban locations. They send paychecks to more remote locations by overnight delivery service.
- *New hire reporting.* Each state government requires a company to report the hiring of new employees to them, so that they can determine if there are any garnishments outstanding against these individuals. Payroll suppliers usually offer this reporting service free of charge.
- *Pay cards.* Larger payroll suppliers offer payroll debit cards as a payment option. This is a good alternative to direct deposit for those employees who do not have bank accounts.
- *Pension plan linkage.* Some payroll suppliers either operate their own 401(k) pension plans or are linked to such plans offered by third parties. These suppliers can link pension deductions in the payroll system to their plans, so no separate pension remittances are required.
- *Reporting.* Suppliers have a standard set of "canned" payroll reports, and usually offer report writing software that allows a user to extract information and present it in formats that are specific to an employer.
- *Software updates.* The employer no longer has to maintain any payroll software in-house, and so is no longer concerned with software updates. The supplier is responsible for all updates to its own software.
- *Tax remittances.* A supplier calculates all payroll taxes and remits them to the government without the company having to be involved. The savings from avoided tax remittance penalties may pay for the entire cost of the supplier.
- *Tax tables.* Suppliers maintain the most up-to-date records of tax rates charged by all government entities, and so can accurately calculate taxes payable to cities, counties, states, the federal government, and other special entities throughout the country.
- *W-2 forms.* All suppliers provide W-2 forms to employees after the end of each calendar year. Many also store this information on-line, so that employees can access their forms from previous years.
- *Other services.* Some suppliers offer additional services related to payroll, such as pension plans, benefits administration, and timekeeping systems.

Thus, there are a broad range of services available to a company that is willing to outsource its payroll function. The key factors are enhanced convenience and the elimination of any risk associated with not remitting payroll taxes on a timely basis.

Reasons Not to Outsource Payroll

There are some situations where using a payroll supplier is not viable or is not cost-effective. These situations are:

- *Cost.* Despite what the payroll suppliers may say, outsourcing payroll is more expensive than processing it in-house, because the supplier has marketing costs and a profit requirement that an in-house payroll department does not have. Suppliers give the appearance of having low-cost services by selling a basic bundle of services at a low cost, and then adding high fees for additional services.
- *Database linkage.* Outsourcing payroll shifts the payroll database to the supplier. This can be a problem when a company is maintaining a large, integrated database of information and needs to have this information in-house.

These two factors are less critical for smaller businesses, which therefore form the core group that outsource payroll. Larger companies are more likely to retain payroll in-house, since they can process payroll at lower cost than suppliers, and can retain payroll information within their computer systems.

Summary

Payroll is one of the most important functions that a trucking firm must address on an ongoing basis, since its revenues are generated by a group of drivers, dispatchers, and maintenance personnel who must be paid correctly and on time – or else they will go to work for a competitor. For a deep analysis of the payroll function, see the author's *Payroll Management* book.

Chapter 4
Accounting Record Keeping

Introduction

A trucking business creates many types of records. A *record* is stored information used as evidence and information, and which has value by being retained for a certain period of time. The more obvious examples are invoices arriving from suppliers or being sent to customers, each one designed to specify the amount owed by the recipient. There are many other types of records, such as:

- *Cash receipts.* A receipt is given to a customer who pays with cash or a credit card.
- *Customer contracts.* Companies enter into formal contracts with their suppliers and customers, detailing the terms and conditions of jobs.
- *Customer records.* A company maintains an ongoing accounts receivable record of the billings issued to a customer and the amounts that the customer has paid to the company.
- *Employee manuals.* A company creates an employee manual, which sets forth all employee-related policies and employment issues.
- *Remittance advices.* A customer prints a check to pay for an invoice, and mails in both the check and a remittance advice that details which invoices are being paid.
- *Tax returns.* A business compiles tax returns, as well as the working papers used as the basis for the information in the tax returns.
- *Timesheets.* An employee completes a timesheet that lists her hours worked each day, and submits it to the bookkeeper, which will convert it into a payment.
- *Titles to property.* An organization may have title documents for any land, buildings, vehicles, and so forth that it owns.

In each of these situations, a record of some kind is created as part of the ongoing operations of a business. One of the most crucial aspects of a record management system is the method used to file records. The method chosen has an impact on the speed of filing and retrievals, as well as the rate of mis-files. In this chapter, we focus on the alphabetic and subject storage systems.

Alphabetic Storage

The most common method for filing records is to arrange them in accordance with the letters of the alphabet. This is quite a simple storage method, since only a knowledge of the alphabetical ordering of records is needed to access files. While alphabetic storage might seem obvious, a set of rules must be constructed and followed religiously in order to ensure that records can be consistently and expeditiously filed and re-trieved.

To properly store a record under an alphabetic storage system, you should engage in the following steps:

Step 1 – Indexing. The individual involved in the storage process must determine the filing segment used to index a record. A *filing segment* is the name under which a record is both stored and later requested by users. This filing segment is then used to place the record in alphabetical order. This initial step is critical, for the person must accurately determine the filing segment every time. Otherwise, an incorrect filing segment might be used, resulting in incorrect record storage that essentially results in the loss of a record, since it is not located where you might reasonably expect it to be. Examples of filing segments are:

- The name of a supplier, when storing a supplier invoice
- The name of an employee, when storing an employee file
- The number of a job, when storing a job record

When selecting a filing segment, the key issue is to use the one most likely to be used in the future when someone requests the record.

Step 2 – Cross-referencing. In some cases, a physical record is likely to be called by two or more names. In these situations, a cross-reference must be created. A cross-reference presents a different name than the one used for the original record; it is used to state the location of the original record. With the careful use of cross-references, it is much more likely that a user can locate a record. Cross-references may not be necessary for electronic records, since database search tools can search entire documents.

A copy of a document may be stored in the cross-reference location, or a sheet containing the cross-reference can be prepared and inserted in the records at the relevant location.

> **Tip:** Limit the use of cross-referencing, since it takes extra time to document each cross-reference, and too many of them can clutter the files.

There are several situations in which a cross-reference may be needed for a business name. They are:

- *Abbreviated names*. When a business is known by an abbreviated name or an acronym, prepare a cross-reference that spells out the full business name.

EXAMPLE

IBM is the abbreviation for International Business Machines. The cross-reference for the firm would be:

International Business Machines

SEE IBM

- *Changed names.* A company may change its name. If so, prepare a cross-reference that traces back to the original company name.

EXAMPLE

The board of directors of Hazardous Garbage Products decides that the company name is not helping its business, and so decides to change the name to Smiley Products. The trucking company that services the new Smiley Products creates the following cross-reference:

Smiley Products

See Hazardous Garbage Products

- *Compound names.* A firm name may include the surnames of several founders. If so, create a cross-reference for each of these names, so that someone can access the relevant record from any one name.

EXAMPLE

A bookkeeper is preparing a supplier file for the company's law firm, which is Hickes, Dwight & Dunn. The two related cross-references that he creates are:

Dwight Dunn and Hickes

SEE Hickes Dwight and Dunn

Dunn Hickes and Dwight

SEE Hickes Dwight and Dunn

- *Similar names.* There are cases in which a business name could be split apart or aggregated through common usage, with a result that differs from the actual company name. If so, prepare a cross-reference for each possible common usage variation on the business name.

EXAMPLE

Northeast Burgers is a customer's name, but common usage could result in the name instead being recorded as North East Burgers. This results in the following cross-reference:

North East Burgers

SEE Northeast Burgers

Step 3 – Sorting. When physical records are being used, the next step in an alphabetic storage system is to arrange the records in the sequence indicated in the preceding coding stage. We note a number of rules for sorting. The key issues to remember when sorting business names are as follows:

- *Business names*. Business names are sorted as written, so there is no presumption that a "last name" within a business name is indexed first. Instead, the first word in the name is assumed to be the filing segment.
- *Business names containing personal names*. If there is a personal name within a business name (such as "Adam's Best Burgers"), sorting is still by the first name.
- *Acronyms*. An acronym is assigned a single filing unit. Thus, the radio station WBEZ is treated as a single filing segment, as would IBM.
- *Punctuation*. Punctuation is omitted for sorting purposes. For example, "Charley's Burgers" is sorted as though it were spelled "Charleys Burgers". Similarly, "D'Angelo" is sorted as though it were spelled "DAngelo". As another example, "Inter-Mountain Express" is sorted as though it were spelled "InterMountain Express."
- *Symbols*. When a symbol appears in a business name, it is spelled out. For example, "$" is sorted as though it were spelled as "Dollar" and "&" is treated as "and". Further, "@" is treated as "at" while "%" is treated as "percent".
- *The*. When the word "The" is used as the first word of a business name, it is considered to be sorted last. For example, "The Wine Place" is treated as "Wine Place, The."

Additional Alphabetic Storage Rules – Business Names

There are several additional rules that apply to the sorting of business names, which are:

- *Numbers spelled out*. When a business spells out a number within its name, the spelled-out number is used for sorting purposes. Examples are "Three Little Pigs Construction" and Two Rivers Condominiums".
- *Numbers as digits*. When numbers appear in a business name as digits, they are sorted before numbers that have been spelled out. Thus, "Number 1 Bakery" appears before "Number One Bakery". Also, numbers are sorted in ascending order, so that "21 Jump Street" appears before "22 Jump Street".

- *Additional numeric designators.* When a number ends in *nd*, *rd*, or *st*, ignore these extra letters and only sort based on the numbers. For example, "1st," "2nd," and "3rd" are treated as 1, 2, and 3.
- *Hyphen separation.* When hyphens are used to separate multiple numbers, remove the hyphens. Thus, "1-2-3 Delivery Service" becomes "123 Delivery Service". Similarly, when names are hyphenated with a number, remove the hyphen. For example, "A-1 Lawn Mowing" becomes "A1 Lawn Mowing".

Problems with Alphabetic Storage

Though alphabetic storage is a dominant storage system, it does suffer from a few problems. In particular, it is quite possible that records will not be filed correctly if users are not thoroughly conversant in the filing rules being used. Also, once a record has been mis-filed, it is extremely difficult to locate it again. Further, it can be easy to mix records when the correspondent names are quite similar. Thus, a record for A.B. Smith could easily be stored in a folder for A.C. Smith.

For these reasons, it is critical to have a well-trained and diligent group of employees. Whenever there is employee turnover, this presents the risk that the incoming person does not have a sufficiently high skill level with the storage system, and so will cause filing problems that may not be detected for some time.

Subject Storage

Though the alphabetic storage system described in the preceding sections is the predominant method in use, this type of records management is usually positioned underneath a subject (by topic) sort. For example, an accounting department will segregate its supplier invoices and customer invoices into separate accounts payable and accounts receivable topics, and then set up an alphabetic storage system underneath these separate topics. As additional examples, a company may separately store records under customer jobs, employee records, and fixed asset records.

One way to set up a records storage system by subject is to sort the topics in alphabetical order. This approach works well when there are not too many records to store, as would be the case with a small trucking business. The following table shows such a filing system.

Sample Subject Storage System in Alphabetical Order

Letter	Subject Tabs
B	Banking
	Budget and Plans
C	Cell phones
	Customer Service
E	Employee Hire Dates
F	Fixed Asset Listings
G	Government Regulations
J	Job Applications
M	Maintenance Records
O	Office Supplies
P	Payroll Information
Q	Quarterly Financial Statements
S	Sales Summaries
T	Tax Filings
	Time Sheets
	Trucks
V	Vacation Schedule
W	W-2 Forms

A different approach is to create a system in which records are filed under a topic and subtopic system. Under this approach, topics are still sorted in alphabetical order, but the emphasis is entirely on topics. For this reason, the main topic is printed on each folder tab, with the sub-topic listed below it. Also, a general topic folder is included at the end of a set of folders under a topic, which is used to accumulate all records that are not assigned to an individual folder. This general topic folder plays the same role as a general folder in an alphabetic record management system. The following exhibit shows such a filing system.

Sample Topic and Sub-Topic Storage System

Topic	Topic and Sub-Topic
Banking	Banking Credit Card Processing
	Banking Fuel Cards
	Banking Procurement Cards
	Banking General Folder
Personnel	Personnel Job Applications
	Personnel Union Agreements
	Personnel W-2 Forms
	Personnel General Folder

A good way to differentiate the tabs in a topic and sub-topic storage system is to assign a specific color to each topic and its associated sub-topics. For example, the banking topic in the preceding example and the four sub-topics associated with it could have red tabs. If one of these folders were to be mis-filed, the associated color would immediately stand out in the filing system.

It is not possible to purchase a pre-configured set of labels for this type of system (as is the case for an alphabetic system), since labels must be custom-created for topics and sub-topics. When creating these labels, use the same font for all labels. If there is a mix of fonts, labels are harder to read, which interferes with the filing and retrieval of records.

Any type of subject records system requires an index. A user first accesses the index to see if a topic exists and where the applicable folder is located, and then goes to the storage system to access the folder. Since this is a two-step process, it is called an indirect access method. An index is usually created and maintained on a computer. The primary indexing format to use is an alphabetic listing of all topics and sub-topics. Consider keeping a recent copy of the index in the records storage area, where it is easily accessible to users. Whenever the index changes, be sure to replace the printed copy in the records storage area with the newest version.

A potential problem with a subject records management system is that documents may need to be perused in detail to ensure that the correct topic and sub-topic are selected. In addition, the most appropriate topic may not yet exist in the records storage system, which may call for additional discussion to determine whether another topic or sub-topic should be created. This can slow down the filing process.

Record Storage Equipment

There are several types of storage equipment used for physical records. They are as follows:

- *Lateral file cabinets.* This is a cabinet in which the width of the unit exceeds its depth. The narrower depth of this arrangement makes these cabinets ideal for storing records in narrower aisles. Hanging folders (as described in the next section) are typically used to store records within each drawer of the cabinet. The sort order can begin at either end, or from front to back. A two-drawer configuration is most convenient for use next to a desk, while four and five-drawer configurations are used for general storage. It requires about one foot of aisle space to pull out a drawer.
- *Vertical file cabinets.* This is a cabinet in which the depth of the unit exceeds its width. Hanging folders are normally used to store records within each drawer of the cabinet. The sort order for the hanging folders is from front to back. A two-drawer configuration is most convenient for use next to a desk, while four and five-drawer configurations are used for general storage. The standard cabinet width is designed to hold letter-size paper, while a wider version is available for legal-size paper. It requires about two feet of aisle space to pull out a drawer.
- *Mobile shelving.* This is a set of shelves that move on tracks in a carousel system, so that a person can access multiple drawers without moving. It is the most expensive type of record storage equipment, but also maximizes the use of available storage space.
- *Shelf files.* This is an open shelf, where records are accessed from the side. It is the least expensive type of record storage equipment. It also requires minimal aisle space, since there is no drawer to pull out. It works well in situations where a large number of files must be frequently retrieved, such as a medical office. However, this is the least secure storage option, since there is no drawer that can be locked to prevent unauthorized access to records.

The type of storage equipment used will depend on the circumstances. When records are confidential, locking cabinets are the best choice. When there is less aisle space available in which to pull out drawers, lateral file cabinets are a good choice. When there is very little storage space available, all options except for vertical file cabinets should be considered. When there is a hefty budget for storage equipment, consider using mobile shelving, since it is the easiest to access and makes the best use of the cubic volume available.

In general, the selection of storage equipment should focus on making the task of accessing records as easy as possible. Most other considerations are secondary to this item.

Record storage is a bad area in which to save money by purchasing inferior or light-duty equipment. Such equipment has a strong tendency to stick, so that drawers do not pull out smoothly (if at all), which incrementally increases the work load of anyone attempting to access records. Instead, this is a good area in which to spend more to obtain high-quality, robust equipment.

Record Storage Supplies

A number of supplies can be used in the storage of physical records. In the following sub-sections, we briefly describe each one.

Guides and Special Guides

A *guide* is a rigid cardboard or plastic divider that is used to signal the start of a new section within a group of records. The use of a reasonable number of guides at regular intervals within a filing system makes it easier for people to locate records. The simplest set of guides can be purchased that contains a separate guide for each letter of the alphabet, as well as for the numbers one through nine. More extensive sets of guides can be purchased that incorporate subsets of the alphabet (such as a separate guide for "Mc"). Blank guides can also be purchased, so that company-specific guides can be created. Guide tabs must extend up or to the side, so that they can be easily seen.

A *special guide* is the same as a guide, which indicates sub-levels of information within a record storage location. In the following exhibit, we show guides that signal the start of a new alphabetic section of a record storage system, followed by subdivisions that are indicated by special guides, and within which folders are located. The use of special guides makes it easier for employees to locate the relevant sections of record storage.

Sample Alphabetic Storage System

Guide	Special Guide	Folder
A		
	Alpharetta	
		Alpharetta Welding Supply
		American Gas Providers
		American Interstate Transport Services
	Animal	
		Animal Feedstock Services
		Applewood Farmers' Cooperative
		Atwood Brothers Drone Spraying, Inc.
B		
	Black	
		Black and Tan Scottish Supplies
		Bridle Horse Trainers, International
		Browne & Belvidere Roofing
	Borrow	
		Borrow More Financial Services
		Byway Farm Equipment Rentals

Tabs

A tab is a projection that rises above the edge of a folder or guide, and which contains indexing information.

Folders

A folder is a cardboard container that holds the records in a file. The best folders contain *score marks*, which are indented lines along the bottom edge that can be folded along to expand the storage capacity of the folder. A folder usually contains a tab, on which is pasted the filing segment for the relevant record. Several folder variations are:

- *Top tab*. A top tab folder has a tab extending out of the top of the folder. It is intended for storage in a filing cabinet, where access is from the top.
- *End tab*. An end tab folder has a tab extending from the side of the folder. It is intended for shelf storage, where access is from the side.

There are a number of tab styles that can be applied to both top tab and end tab configurations. A straight cut tab extends across the entire top or side of a folder. A one-third cut means that the tab extends across one-third of the top or side. Similarly, a one-fifth cut means that the tab extends across one-fifth of the top or side. Tabs are commonly placed in a staggered arrangement, starting on the left and progressing to the right. For example, in a one-third cut folder, the first tab position is reserved for the guides, the second tab position is reserved for the special guides, and the third tab position is reserved for the folders. This tab placement is illustrated in the following example, where we employ a compressed version of the preceding exhibit, with an extra row inserted to indicate tab positions.

Sample Alphabetic Storage Tab Positions

Guide	Special Guide	Folder
1st Tab	2nd Tab	3rd Tab
A		
	Alpharetta	
		Alpharetta Welding Supply
B		
	Black	
		Black and Tan Scottish Supplies

Folders may be employed in several ways. A *general folder* contains records that involve small volumes, where there is no need for a specially-designated folder. For example, there is a "C" folder at the end of the "C" section of folders that holds all miscellaneous records. Records are arranged within this folder alphabetically by correspondent name. An *individual folder* is used to store only the records for a specific correspondent; it is typically employed when there is a sufficient volume of records to warrant a separate folder. Records are arranged within this folder by date, with the most recently-dated records first.

The preceding two types of folders were the same physical version of a folder, but used for different purposes. The following are specialized folders that are designed for more specific uses:

- *Bellows folder.* A bellows folder is a free-standing folder that contains a number of built-in dividers. It is used to store records when the total volume of records is quite small. For example, the bookkeeper of a small company might find that a bellows folder is sufficient for storing all unpaid accounts payable.
- *Hanging folder.* A hanging folder contains hooks on each side that are suspended from the rails in a file drawer. Plastic tabs are then added to the upper edge of these folders. General and individual folders are placed within a hanging folder. These folders are highly useful for maintaining an orderly filing system.

Additional Supplies

There are several other supplies that can be of use in a records management system. The *follower block* is a metal plate at the back of a file drawer that can be adjusted to reduce the effective length of the drawer. This adjustment is used to keep folders upright in the front of the drawer. Otherwise, the folders will sag, which can damage them and also makes it more difficult to access folders. A follower block is not needed when hanging folders are used, since these folders are suspended from side rails and so will not slide down.

An *OUT indicator* is a sheet or folder that indicates the location of records that have been removed from storage. This indicator contains space to write in the name of the person who removed the records, the date of the removal, and the due date for its return. There may also be room for a notation regarding the contents of the removed records. The indicator is inserted into the files when records are removed, and is pulled out when the records are returned. To make the indicator easy to find, it may have a bright color, and includes a large tab with the word "OUT" printed on it. Not only is an OUT indicator useful for keeping track of records, it also reduces the work required to find the location in which to re-insert records.

Record Preparation and Filing

There are several steps to take when preparing physical records for storage, so that they are not damaged and can be easily accessed. The steps can be divided into record preparation and record filing, as follows:

Record Preparation

- *Combine documents.* Remove all paper clips being used to fasten documents together. Instead, staple these documents in the upper right corner. The use of this corner means that other records being inserted into a folder will not be accidentally inserted between stapled pages.

- *Repair documents*. Use tape to cover over any document tears. Otherwise, there is a risk that the records will be more extensively torn when filed or removed from folders.

<u>Record Filing</u>

1. *Identify folder*. See if there is an individual folder into which the record can be filed. If not, move to the general folder for the applicable letter range.
2. *Raise folder*. Raise the applicable folder, to ensure that the record is placed in that folder, rather than an adjacent folder.
3. *Position record*. File each record in a folder with its top to the left. By doing so, stapled sets of records have the staple in the top, so that no other records can be inadvertently inserted between them. Also, the most recent record is positioned in the front of the folder.
4. *Replace in order*. When replacing a record in a folder, insert it in the correct chronological sequence, to avoid record jumbling.

Summary

An alphabetic filing system is likely to be the default system adopted in most situations, since it is highly intuitive. The subject filing approach is typically used by somewhat larger organizations with more topics for which filing must be conducted. There is a good chance that an organization may employ a mix of these options, depending on its needs. All of these systems require a good knowledge of filing rules to avoid mis-filings, so the filing staff should be well-trained before being allowed anywhere near the record storage system.

Chapter 5
How to Organize the Business

Introduction

A key administrative activity is to properly organize a trucking firm. This includes the selection of the optimal legal structure, obtaining a variety of licenses, setting up an accounting system, acquiring insurance, and several additional steps. We cover these activities in the following pages.

Legal Structures

There are several legal structures that can be used to organize a trucking business. In this section, we briefly explore the characteristics of each one, so that you can decide which will serve you best. These legal structures are the sole proprietorship, partnership, corporation, and limited liability company.

Sole Proprietorship

In a sole proprietorship, you are the only owner of the business, and you are personally responsible for its obligations. This means that lenders can pursue your personal assets in order to obtain payment on any overdue loans, even if they were incurred specifically for the business (such as to purchase trucks). Furthermore, if a driver is involved in an accident while on company business, the injured party could claim your personal assets in compensation. If any bills go unpaid, then creditors could garnish your wages until they are repaid – which could take years. Realistically, these issues mean that, if your trucking business goes bankrupt, you may have to seek bankruptcy protection yourself.

While the issues just presented will probably persuade you not to use a sole proprietorship structure, there are a few advantages to it. First, as the sole owner, you will have entire authority over all decisions. Second, being the sole owner, you will receive all of the profits. And finally, it requires the least paperwork. Nonetheless, the unlimited liability associated with sole proprietorships makes this a dicey proposition.

Partnership

A partnership is a form of business organization in which the owners have unlimited personal liability for the actions of the business, though this problem can be mitigated through the use of a limited liability partnership. The owners of a partnership have invested their own funds and time in the business, and share proportionately in any profits earned by it. There may also be limited partners in the business, who contribute funds but do not take part in day-to-day operations. A limited partner is only liable for the amounts he or she invests in the business; once those funds are paid out, the limited partner has no additional liability in relation to the activities of the partnership.

Conversely, the general partner who actually runs the business has unlimited personal liability for the obligations of the firm.

Corporation

A corporation is a legal entity whose investors purchase shares of stock as evidence of their ownership interest in it. This entity acts as a legal shield for its owners, which means that they are generally not liable for the corporation's actions, though they can benefit from dividend payments and any appreciation in the value of their shares. This structure works well for larger organizations, where you might want to sell stock to investors in order to raise funds, or issue stock options to employees as an incentive measure. A corporation's shareholders elect a board of directors, who run the firm on their behalf. The board then hires a senior management team that runs the daily operations of the business.

There are some downsides to the corporation structure. A key one is that the business must file its own tax return (which can be complicated), and pay income taxes. If the corporation issues dividends to its shareholders, then they must pay income taxes on the dividends. This is known as double taxation. Another downside is that, when there are many investors with no clear majority interest, the management team can operate the business without any real oversight from the owners. This can lead to a muddied strategy direction for the business, and possibly bloated corporate overhead.

A variation on the corporation concept is the S corporation. An S corporation is a corporate entity that passes its income through to its owners, so that the entity itself does not pay income taxes. The owners report the income on their tax returns, thereby avoiding the double taxation that arises in a regular corporation. In effect, an S corporation entitles shareholders to the protections of incorporation while avoiding double taxation. However, the S corporation structure only allows for the use of one class of stock, (as opposed to the use of both common and preferred stock in a normal corporation). In addition, the number of shareholders in an S corporation is capped at 100.

Limited Liability Company

A limited liability company (LLC) is one of the best forms of organization for a trucking firm. This structure protects your personal assets from the liabilities of the business, so that creditors can only pursue the LLC's assets. They cannot access your personal assets, unless you personally guarantee a loan. In addition, the profits and losses of the LLC are passed straight through to your personal income tax return, rather than being paid by the entity. This can reduce your overall tax filings. A further advantage is that this structure can be used even when you are the sole owner, which makes it a superior choice to a sole proprietorship.

> **Note:** You will have to pay self-employment taxes on any profits passed through to you by an LLC. These taxes include social security and Medicare and total 15.3%, of which 12.4% is for social security and 2.9% for Medicare. Depending on the amount owed, you will likely need to make quarterly self-employment tax payments to the government. A partnership has the same requirement.

Yet another advantage of an LLC, and one which strongly differentiates it from an S corporation, is that you can elect to have the corporation pay taxes, rather than the owners. By doing so, you can retain more cash within the business, which is important when the firm is growing at a rapid clip. Otherwise, when profits are passed through to the owners so that they can pay taxes on it, they will likely demand that the firm's cash be distributed to them too, so that they have enough funds to pay the taxes.

An LLC can also be set up to have multiple owners. If so, the profits and losses of the business are apportioned among the owners in accordance with the terms of an operating agreement. You will only have to pay taxes on that portion of the profits and losses that have been allocated to you.

Which Structure to Choose

The type of legal structure to choose will depend on your specific situation. For example, if you need to raise money from a number of investors, it may be necessary to sell them shares, which calls for some variation on a corporation. Or, if you plan to start the business with your own funds, then a sole-member LLC might be the best choice. Or, if you plan to start up the business with a small number of associates, a multi-member LLC would be a good option. It makes sense to discuss the options with an attorney who is familiar with the state-level requirements for each of these legal structures, so that you can make an informed choice. That being said, the default choice for many truckers is an LLC, since it provides you with protection from the liabilities of the business, and requires only a modest amount of paperwork to maintain.

> **Tip:** No matter which type of legal entity you choose to use, you will need to register it in your home state of operations as a domestic entity, and as a foreign entity in any additional states in which you plan to conduct business.

Obtain an Employer Identification Number

Any business needs an employer identification number (EIN), which is also known as a Federal Tax Identification Number. It is used to uniquely identify a business entity. You can apply for an EIN online, through the website of the Internal Revenue Service (IRS). This is a free service offered by the IRS; once you complete the online form, the IRS automatically grants you an EIN.

The EIN is used to identify the business on any tax forms and licenses, so obtaining it should be one of your first activities to complete.

Obtain a USDOT Number

Companies that haul freight in interstate commerce must be registered with the Federal Motor Carrier Safety Administration (FMCSA) and have a USDOT[2] number. The USDOT number serves as a unique identifier when collecting and monitoring a company's safety information acquired during audits, compliance reviews, crash investigations, and inspections. This number should appear on both sides of the commercial vehicle, and should be legible from 50 feet away in daylight hours (typically meaning that the USDOT number is at least two inches high).

Obtain an MC Authority

An MC Authority is a number assigned by the FMCSA to identify a carrier operating for hire and transporting regulated commodities in interstate commerce. This MC number is also known as an operating authority or trucking authority. You will only need an MC authority if you are starting your own trucking business and will drive as an owner-operator. Independent truck drivers can operate under the MC authority of another company, and so do not need to register separately. The following steps must be completed in order to obtain an MC Authority:

1. Create a business entity
2. Apply for MC Authority
3. Get a USDOT number
4. Designate a process agent
5. Obtain a Universal Carrier Registration permit
6. Pay the heavy vehicle use tax
7. Set up an International Fuel Tax Agreement account
8. Enroll in a drug and alcohol testing program

This is an expensive, multi-month process.

Set Up a Checking Account

No matter which legal structure you choose for your trucking firm, it will absolutely need its own checking account. There are several reasons for doing so. One (and the most important) is that you need to maintain a high degree of separation between your personal finances and those of the business, where your personal affairs are linked to a personal bank account, and your business's operations are conducted through a separate account. Otherwise, if these transactions were to be mixed together in a single account, there is a good chance that a creditor could convince a court to access your personal assets to satisfy the debts of the business.

> **Tip:** Set up the account to have an end-of-month cutoff date, so that the bank's monthly statement matches the period used for the company's financial statements.

---

[2] U.S. Department of Transportation

The same concept applies if you decide to open several branches of the business. Each one should have its own checking account, so that you can more clearly differentiate the cash flows for that part of the business.

Another reason to have a separate checking account is to keep control over the business checking account out of the hands of any family members who might have check writing privileges on your personal account. This can be crucial when a spend-thrift family member wants to extract a large amount of cash from the business without authorization.

> **Tip:** If the business generates a reasonable amount of excess cash, consider shifting this excess into a separate savings or money market account. Doing so will generate a small return, and will also segregate the cash from the checking account, so that no one can illicitly access the cash with a fraudulent check.

Obtain a Company Credit Card

An excellent way to reduce the amount of accounting paperwork is to pay for as many business expenditures as possible with a separate company credit card. By doing so, you can replace a large number of individual payment transactions with one large one, all neatly organized for you on a credit card statement.

> **Tip:** It is acceptable to issue additional credit cards to the staff, but monitor their usage of these cards, and be willing to withdraw the privilege if there is any evidence of misuse.

Some credit card providers will let you download a file that provides the details for your purchases, so that you can manipulate the figures in an electronic spreadsheet. This makes it much easier to create a journal entry that aggregates the various expenditures and logs them into the correct account.

> **Tip:** Budget for the projected amount of your monthly credit card bill, so that you will always have sufficient cash on hand to pay the full amount. This is critical, since the interest rates on credit cards can be stratospheric.

Set Up Payment Receipt Methods

Customers may want to pay your business through a variety of approaches – it is no longer just by check. That means you will need to consider setting up a credit card payment application on your computer, perhaps through Stripe or PayPal, as well as such financial services apps as Venmo or Zelle. It may be easier to begin with cash and check payments, and then wait to see if any customers demand other payment methods. If you decide to offer credit card payments, be aware that the credit card processing services will charge fees that are generally in the range of 3-4% of the amount being paid, which can seriously reduce your profits.

> **Tip:** Even if you accept credit card payments, do not publicize this service. If customers are not aware of it, they will be more likely to pay by less expensive means.

Be aware that credit card processors will likely take a few business days to credit your account when a customer pays with a credit card, which might have a negative impact on your projected cash flows.

Acquire Accounting Software

There are a number of accounting software packages that are targeted specifically at trucking operations. Examples of these packages are Quickbooks Online with TruckingOffice Integration, Tailwind TMS, Rigbooks, Axon, and Q7. Any of these packages allow you to keep all accounting transactions in a central database, while also tracking employee hours worked, issue billings to customers, record supplier invoices, and reconcile your bank accounts. These packages also contain report writers that allow you to print out a complete set of pre-configured financial statements. And, as noted in the next section, accounting software will keep track of your supplier invoices, so that you know exactly when each one is due for payment.

These more specialized software packages are especially useful for tracking the gallons of fuel purchased for all qualified vehicles in your fleet for each jurisdiction (tax paid gallons). This information is needed for your quarterly International Fuel Tax Agreement (IFTA) reporting to the applicable state governments where your trucks conduct operations.

Plan for Supplier Payments

One thing you do not want to do is get behind on your payments to suppliers. If you do, they will eventually cut off your credit, forcing you to pay cash for everything – which may trigger a cash crunch that takes down your business. To avoid this, buy an accounting software package, and load every supplier invoice into it as soon as it arrives. By doing so, you can print out an aged accounts payable report that tells you exactly when every supplier invoice is due. With this tool in hand, you can more easily plan for the cash needed to make payments to suppliers on a timely basis.

> **Tip:** Whenever you receive a late fee from a supplier, stop and figure out why it happened. Chances are, you were missing a key procedure or control that allowed that supplier's invoice to slip through the cracks and not be paid.

Designate a Bookkeeper

A common problem for the founders of small trucking firms is that they try to handle every accounting chore themselves. A usual outcome is that the accounting task is given a low priority in comparison to the multitude of other concerns, so that billings, expenses, and cash in general are not monitored as closely as they should be. As a result, you may find that your inattention to the accounting aspects of the business will destroy it. Consequently, a reasonable decision is to initially bring in a bookkeeper – even if only on a part-time basis – to keep a close watch over the accounting. You will have to pay for this person's compensation, but offsetting this expense is the security of knowing that someone is maintaining the books better that you could have done.

Having a bookkeeper is a good start, but also engage the services of a CPA, who can review your books following the end of the year and suggest improvements that can save you money for the next year. At a minimum, the CPA should certainly be able to offer tax advice that can be of assistance, and can represent you if you are ever hit with a tax audit.

Explore Financing Options

If your business does not have a large amount of cash on hand, it may be difficult to meet the ongoing obligations of the business, such as paying employees and suppliers. This is a particular concern in the trucking industry, where it can take 30 to 90 days to be paid under the typical shipping contract. With such delayed cash inflows, many trucking firms have a difficult time paying their bills.

A possible financing option for dealing with this situation is *factoring*, which is when a lender buys your company's accounts receivable at a discount. The terms can vary, but the general approach is for your business to sell its receivables in exchange for about 70% to 85% of the face value of each invoice, plus a fee that ranges from 2% to 5% of the face amount of the invoice. Once the factor collects payment on the invoice, it remits back to you the difference between the face value of the invoice and the amount of cash already provided (less the fee already noted). This arrangement is, in essence, a loan with a high interest rate. For example, assume a 3% fee on a $1,000 invoice, with only 80%, or $800, of cash actually paid to the company up front. The fee is therefore $30 to use $800 for the typical 30-day term of an invoice, which is an annualized borrowing rate of 45% (calculated as 30×12 months, divided by $800). In short, the main benefit of factoring is a near-immediate receipt of cash for outstanding invoices, while the main downside is the cost of the arrangement.

> **Note:** Factoring for the trucking industry is quite advanced, and has its own name, which is freight factoring. Some factoring agencies go so far as to issue bills for you and follow up on late payments, while also providing free credit checks on your customers. In essence, you are outsourcing your receivables function to another firm.

There are two types of factoring, which are recourse factoring and non-recourse factoring. Under recourse factoring, you will be responsible for paying back the factor if a customer does not pay for an invoice you sold to the factor. Factors charge lower fees for this arrangement, but you will have the risk of taking back non-performing invoices. Under a non-recourse arrangement, the factor is fully responsible for collection of each invoice, and will have to write it off if the customer will not pay. Given the greater risks undertaken by the factor in the latter arrangement, it should be no surprise that the cost of this arrangement can be substantially higher than for recourse factoring.

Tip: If your customers have relatively poor payment records, it may be impossible to enter into a factoring arrangement, since the factor does not want to waste time badgering them to pay their invoices.

Tip: Read the fine print for any factoring arrangement before agreeing to it. Some factoring companies add on transaction and other fees that can increase the financing cost substantially.

Given the high cost of factoring, it can make sense to treat it as a secondary financing source that backs up less-expensive options. A lower-cost option for a trucking firm is asset-based lending, where your company assets are used as collateral in order to secure a loan. For a trucking firm, this usually means that the lender wants to use your accounts receivable and truck assets as collateral. Because the existence of collateral lowers the lender's risk of nonpayment, it can offer a substantially reduced interest rate on the loan. However, the downside is that, if you can't repay the loan, the lender will take possession of the assets you posted as collateral.

Tip: Many lenders will try to obtain a personal guarantee from you as part of a lending arrangement. Though you may not have any choice in the matter, try to avoid this guarantee, since it allows the lender to take your personal assets in the event of a loan default.

Obtain General Liability Insurance

A key element of organizing a trucking business is making sure that it is properly covered by insurance. The main policy to obtain is commercial general liability insurance. The purpose of this insurance is to protect your firm from losses if it is held liable for causing injuries to others or damage to property owned by a third party. Commercial general liability insurance provides coverage for a number of possible events, such as claims arising from bodily injury, personal injury, and damage to property that is caused by the operations or products of a business.

When a claim is made, the insurer defends the insured. The main types of coverage that can be purchased are:

- *Bodily injury and property damage.* Pays for losses arising from bodily injury or property damage to a third party when the insured entity is legally liable.
- *Personal and advertising injury.* Pays for losses arising from the loss of reputation, humiliation, economic loss, and bodily injury that is caused by several actions by the insured party, including copyright infringement, libel, slander, and wrongful eviction.

- *Medical payments.* Pays for the medical expenses of third parties when an injury was caused by an accident on the premises of the insured party or as a result of the operations of the insured party.

General liability insurance may contain coverage exclusions, so be sure to review the proposed policy with care. A selection of these exclusions follows:

- Criminal acts
- Distribution of materials in violation of statutes
- Intended injuries
- Material published prior to policy period
- Use of electronic chatrooms or bulletin boards

Another consideration when buying this type of insurance is to determine whether it is a claims-made or occurrence policy. A *claims-made* policy only provides coverage for claims made during a specific date range. An *occurrence* policy provides coverage for events occurring within a specific date range. Thus, a claims-made policy focuses on the date of the claim, while an occurrence policy focuses on the date of the triggering event.

Some customers may require that their suppliers have commercial general liability insurance, especially when large contracts are involved, so this is usually considered a mandatory type of insurance.

Coverage Limitations

Liability limits will be set for each individual policy. For example, a policy may state that there is a $100,000 limit per personal injury occurrence and $250,000 per property damage occurrence. The insured party would be liable for any losses above these limits. When there is a per occurrence limit, this means that the amount paid by the insurer is limited to the designated amount for an occurrence, irrespective of the number of claims received from all affected parties that arose from that occurrence.

An alternative form of coverage limitation is for the insurer to set a single aggregate liability limit, irrespective of the number of occurrences. Once claims are paid up to this limit, the insurer will not pay out any additional amounts during the policy year.

Umbrella Coverage

Umbrella coverage is a separate policy that provides an extra tranche of coverage for a general liability policy. It is not activated unless a loss exceeds the per occurrence or aggregate limits on the underlying liability policy. The underlying coverage must be maintained for the umbrella coverage to take effect.

Obtain Commercial Property Insurance

Commercial property insurance protects against the loss of physical assets. If you have acquired assets (such as trucks) with asset-based loans, the lienholders will require that property insurance be purchased in order to protect their interests in the assets. This is usually considered essential insurance, since it provides coverage of what may be the largest assets of a business.

Types of Property

The coverage given by property insurance applies to two types of property, which are real property and personal property. *Real property* is defined as any property that is directly attached to the land, plus land itself. Examples are buildings and storage units, as well as improvements to these structures. *Personal property* is defined as being movable, and so may include furniture and fixtures, vehicles, and collectibles.

Policy Inclusions

There are three different classifications of damage to property that may be covered by property insurance, depending on the type of coverage purchased. The three classifications are as follows:

- *Causes of loss – basic form.* Coverage is provided when the causes of loss include fire, lightning, windstorms, hail, riots, damage by aircraft or vehicles, smoke, explosion, vandalism, volcanism, a sinkhole collapse, or discharge from an automatic sprinkler system.
- *Causes of loss – broad form.* Coverage is provided for all of the perils just noted for the basic form, as well as for falling objects, weight of snow, ice, or sleet, and water damage.
- *Causes of loss – special form.* Coverage is provided for all types of accidental loss, unless there is a specific exclusion.

Damage due to flooding and earthquakes is typically excluded from all property insurance policies, but can be added back as a separate endorsement to a policy.

Property is covered if it is located within 100 feet of the insured premises. Additional coverage can be obtained that provides coverage at other locations, as well as for newly acquired or constructed property that is obtained after the effective date of the policy.

Personal property owned by third parties is also included in the insurance coverage, if this property is in the custody of the insured party and is located on the premises.

Policy Exclusions

A number of items are specifically excluded from a property insurance policy. Depending on the policy, exclusions may encompass the following:

- *Cash and securities.* This includes bills and coins, bonds, and equity securities.
- *Land and land improvements.* This includes roadways, lawns, bridges, underground pipes, patios, roadways, pilings, and parking lots.

- *Plants and outdoor property.* This includes crops, lawns, shrubs, trees, antennas and signs.
- *Vehicles.* This exclusion applies except when the vehicles are being manufactured, held for sale, or stored.
- *Covered elsewhere.* This includes property that is more specifically addressed under another insurance policy.

Obtain Cargo Insurance

Cargo insurance covers the freight being hauled. This coverage is required by the risk managers of larger customers. It covers the firm's liability for cargo that is lost or damaged due to such causes as fire or collision. The removal expenses portion of this coverage will pay for the removal of debris or the extraction of pollutants, if a load is accidentally dumped on a roadway or waterway. It also pays for the costs related to the prevention of further loss to damaged cargo.

When purchasing cargo insurance, you can select a limit for the amount of coverage you want. The limit determines the maximum amount that the insurer will pay for damaged or destroyed cargo. You can also select the deductible amount; picking a higher deductible will lower the cost of the insurance, but will increase your out-of-pocket cost whenever there is a claim.

Cargo insurance is only available for for-hire trucking risks on policies with trailers or flatbeds (which covers most trucking operations). Some cargo types are excluded from this coverage, including art, cash, pharmaceuticals, alcohol, live animals, property not stated on a bill of lading, shipping containers, and explosive or radioactive material.

Summary

All of the activities listed in this chapter should be considered essential to the organization of a trucking business; you cannot skip any steps. Without a proper legal structure, you will take on significant personal liability for the activities of the business. Without licenses, your trucks will not be allowed on the road. And without insurance, almost any incident can cause losses large enough to bankrupt the firm. And finally, an accounting system is needed to keep track of what is happening and report results back to you.

Chapter 6
Cost Controls

Introduction

The majority of newly-established trucking firms fail within a short period of time, usually because their owners did not pay sufficient attention to the costs being incurred. In this chapter, we cover the basic concepts for monitoring your costs, and provide specific suggestions for how to keep your costs low and cash flows high.

Understand Your Fixed Costs

A key step in the process of controlling your costs is understanding your fixed costs. A *fixed cost* is a cost that does not increase or decrease in conjunction with any activities. It must be paid on a recurring basis, even when there is no business activity. A prime example would be the rent on your business premises, as well as the rent on the land where you are parking the firm's vehicles. Another might be a lease on a truck, where you are required to pay a minimum amount per month. Other fixed costs might include the monthly plan on your cell phones, the minimum utility charge on the company's premises, and the monthly liability insurance bill. These costs must be covered on an ongoing basis, or the company will not make money. Therefore, once you understand your fixed costs, the next step is to devise the breakeven point for the business, which we cover shortly.

Understand Your Contribution Margin

The *contribution margin* is a service's price minus all variable costs, resulting in the incremental profit earned for each unit of service provided. The total contribution margin generated represents the total earnings available to pay for fixed costs and generate a profit.

Note: Examples of the variable costs incurred by a trucking business are fuel, truck maintenance, tolls, and replacement tires, as well as driver meals and lodging.

The measure is useful for determining whether to allow a lower price in special pricing situations. If the contribution margin is excessively low or negative, it would be unwise to continue selling a service at that price point. It is also useful for determining the profits that will arise from various sales levels (see the next example).

To determine the amount of contribution margin for a service, subtract all variable costs of the service from its revenues, and divide by its revenue. The calculation is:

$$\frac{\text{Service revenue} - \text{Service variable costs}}{\text{Service revenue}}$$

EXAMPLE

Iverson Trucking has entered into a deal with a local manufacturer and its supplier, where Iverson commits to make a just-in-time delivery of parts from the supplier to the manufacturer six times a day, for $500 per day. In the most recent month, it provided this service on 22 days, for a total billing of $11,000. Offsetting this revenue was fuel and maintenance costs (the variable cost component) of $4,000, as well as the $8,000 salary and benefits of the driver (the fixed cost component). The result appears in the following table.

Revenue	$11,000
Variable expenses	4,000
Contribution margin	7,000
Fixed expenses	8,000
Net loss	-$1,000

Iverson's contribution margin is 64%, so if it wants to break even, the company needs to either reduce its fixed expenses by $1,000 or increase its sales by $1,563 (calculated as the $1,000 loss divided by the 64% contribution margin).

Understand Your Breakeven Point

The *breakeven point* is the sales volume at which a business earns exactly no money, where all contribution margin earned is needed to pay for the firm's fixed costs. The concept is most easily illustrated in the following chart, where fixed costs occupy a block of expense at the bottom of the table, irrespective of any sales being generated. Variable costs are incurred in concert with the sales level. Once the contribution margin on each sale cumulatively matches the total amount of fixed costs, the breakeven point has been reached. All sales above that level directly contribute to profits.

Breakeven Table

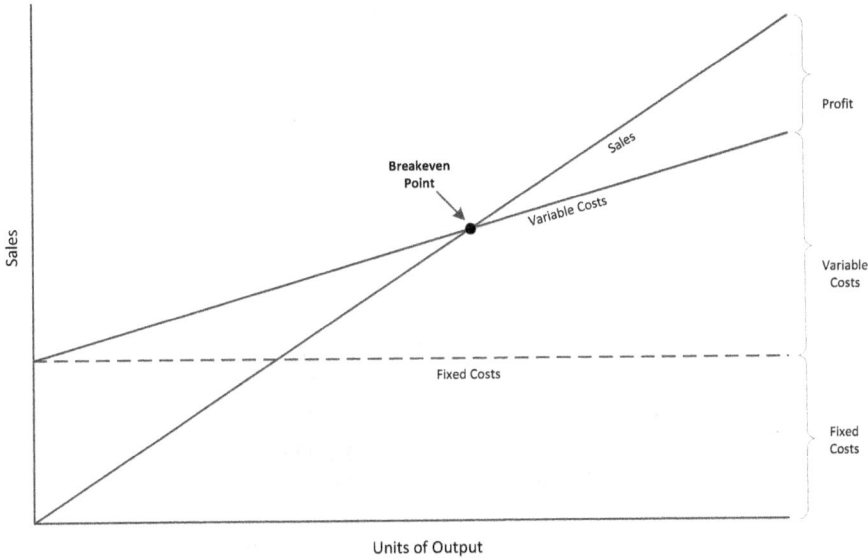

Knowledge of the breakeven point is useful for the following reasons:

- Determining the amount of remaining capacity after the breakeven point is reached, which reveals the maximum amount of profit that can be generated.
- Determining the change in profits if trucking prices are altered.
- Determining the amount of losses that could be sustained if the business suffers a sales downturn.

In addition, the breakeven concept is useful for establishing the overall ability of a business to generate a profit. When the breakeven point is near its maximum sales level, this means it is nearly impossible to earn a profit even under the best of circumstances.

You should constantly monitor the breakeven point, particularly in regard to the last item noted, in order to reduce the breakeven point whenever possible. Ways to do this include:

- *Cost analysis.* Continually review all fixed costs, to see if any can be eliminated. Also review variable costs to see if they can be eliminated, since doing so increases margins and reduces the breakeven point.
- *Margin analysis.* Pay close attention to service margins, and push sales of the highest-margin items, thereby reducing the breakeven point.
- *Outsourcing.* If an activity involves a fixed cost, consider outsourcing it in order to turn it into a per-unit variable cost, which reduces the breakeven point.

- *Pricing.* Reduce or eliminate the use of price reductions, since they increase the breakeven point.
- *Technologies.* Implement any technologies that can improve the efficiency of the business, thereby increasing capacity with no increase in cost.

To calculate the breakeven point, divide total fixed expenses by the contribution margin (which was described earlier). The formula is:

$$\frac{\text{Total fixed expenses}}{\text{Contribution margin percentage}}$$

A more refined approach is to eliminate all non-cash expenses (such as depreciation) from the numerator, so that the calculation focuses on the breakeven cash flow level. The formula is:

$$\frac{\text{Total fixed expenses} - \text{Depreciation}}{\text{Contribution margin percentage}}$$

Knowing your breakeven point makes it easier to decide whether it makes sense to take on additional work, perhaps involving the addition of more trucks.

EXAMPLE

Milford Trucking has grown rapidly, and has consistently generated a reasonable profit by ensuring that it only takes on well-priced work. The owner, Jeffrey Davidson, has recently been offered a one-year contract to provide services to a major new customer, for which he estimates that the billing will be $240,000 per year. He estimates that the contribution margin on this work will be 30%, and that the fixed costs of the trucks he will need to lease for this contract will be $80,000 per year. This results in the following calculation:

$80,000 Total fixed expenses ÷ 30% Contribution margin = $266,667 Breakeven point

Based on this information, he should reject the proposed contract, on the grounds that it is guaranteed to generate losses. He might consider counter-offering with a higher price that will earn Milford a reasonable profit, probably somewhere around $300,000 in billings per year.

Tip: Be aware of the breakeven number of miles that must be driven each month. This is the minimum number of miles that must be driven in order to cover your monthly expenditures.

Follow a Budget

Setting up a budget gives you a spending target. As long as the business does not spend more than what is listed in the budget (and assuming that revenue levels are achieved), then you will end up somewhere near the budgeted profit. Though reality can diverge enormously from the expectations codified in your budget, simply having one provides a massive control. Whenever an expenditure is made, reduce the budgeted expense in that category by the same amount, which tells you how much you can afford to spend for the rest of the year. Without this standard, there is a good chance that expenditures will take off, resulting in unexpected losses by year-end.

A further advantage of having a budget is that it forces you to set up financial goals for the business. Doing so can be quite informative, since you will gain a more realistic view of how much the business can earn, how fast it can grow, how much debt it can take on, and so forth. Furthermore, having a budget is a useful tool for obtaining a bank loan, since the lender can use it to review your assumptions regarding future revenues, expenses, and debts.

> **Tip:** Initially, revise your budget every month, until you have enough consistent financial performance to attempt a longer-term budget. If your results still vary by a large amount over time, then keep the budget duration fairly short, perhaps in the vicinity of just the next three months.

A useful enhancement to a budget is to include in it those expenses that are relatively infrequent, such as computer replacements or a major engine overhaul. You may not be able to predict exactly when these expenses will be incurred, but a rough guess at the timing will give you a better idea of whether some major expenses are looming somewhere in the not-too-distant future.

Track Costs on a Trend Line

A good way to spot sudden increases in costs is to track them on a trend line by month. Many accounting software packages offer this reporting format, where the income statement for every month of the year is presented in adjacent columns. Then use a ruler to work your way down the report, examining expenses incurred by line item, by month. If there is a sudden spike in an expense, then drill down to the underlying source document to figure out what happened. By conducting this cost review each month, you will have a better awareness of how your expenses are changing over time – and may find some expenses that can be reduced or even eliminated.

Track Costs and Profits by Job

The ultimate performance benchmark is whether a job earns a profit. You can do this by accumulating costs by job, such as the costs of fuel, tolls, food, lodging, and compensation, and then subtracting these costs from the associated job revenue to arrive at a profit or loss. Doing so provides great information about whether you underestimated the costs that would be incurred for a job, or whether it was underpriced. This information can be used to provide proposed prices to customers on future jobs that are more likely to consistently generate a profit for the business.

Standardize the Contract

A good way to reduce conflicts with customers over billed amounts is to develop a standard transport contract, using the same terms for all customers. This can be initially developed from a template, but consider adjusting it over time to deal with any problems you have encountered. Once a customer signs this contract, file it properly, so that it can be readily accessed in the event of a dispute. With clearly stated terms and conditions, a signed contract leaves difficult customers little wiggle room in trying to negotiate down the amount of an invoice.

Add a Fuel Surcharge

To protect your profits from sudden spikes in fuel prices over the course of a job, add a clause to the contract that allows you to charge customers a fuel surcharge when prices spike above a certain level. Doing so passes the loss through to customers, allowing you to maintain your planned profits.

Review Billings

Job billings are an easy place in which to make mistakes. If you mistakenly bill too much, then the customer will probably bring up the issue, or at least refuse to pay. However, if you underbill a customer, it is quite unlikely that the other party will complain. Consequently, it can make sense to review your own billings, or have a second person manually check each one. This is a worthwhile activity, even if you only make a mistake one time out of a hundred.

> **Tip:** Send invoices to customers as soon as a job is finished. Doing so gives the customer no excuse to delay payment on the grounds that it never received your invoice.

Collect, Collect, Collect

Many small trucking firms are not well funded, so any shortfall in cash flow can shut them down with little warning. The single best way to avoid this issue is to ensure that every invoiced customer pays on time. To make that this happens, give customers just a few days grace period after the due date on your invoices, and then start calling them. Make note of what they promise, and call back on those promised pay dates, to discuss why payments have not yet been made. Only by developing a reputation for following up on overdue invoices will customers begin to respect the due dates on your invoices.

> **Tip:** Set up a routine for calling customers every day. Block out time on your calendar for it. Otherwise, the annoyance of this task tends to drive it down your priority list, so that it's rarely done at all.

> **Tip:** Create a standard script for what to say to a customer during a collection call, as well as a standard collection text for emails. This reduces the time required to make collection calls.

> **Tip:** Offer customers an early payment discount of a few percent in exchange for paying within ten days of the invoice date. This gives them enough time to receive the invoice in the mail and process it through their accounting system.

> **Tip:** Offer to take credit card payments. You will have to absorb a 3-5% credit card fee, but this approach makes it easier for customers to pay, and may eliminate some invoices that would otherwise have turned into bad debts.

Drop Below-Standard Customers

Some customers are not ideal. They are demanding, find issues with your invoices, and try to bargain down the price once a job has already been invoiced. Or, some customers are deeply apologetic about late payments – but those payments are still late, sometimes by quite a few months. You should weed out both types of customers. Doing so leaves more capacity to take on new customers who may be better business partners, and also eliminates the ongoing annoyance of having to deal with late payments.

> **Tip:** Run a credit report on new customers before doing any work with them, and turn them down if the credit report is sub-standard. Credit reports are devised from the reporting of other businesses in their dealings with these customers, and so are a good way to spot difficult prospective customers.

The same concept applies to brokers. Some load boards[3] include the credit scores of freight brokers. If a broker has a poor credit score, it makes sense to avoid the jobs it has posted, on the grounds that the associated payment could be a long time in coming.

Use a Fuel Card

A fuel card is used as a payment card for the purchase of gasoline, diesel, and other fuels at gas stations. These cards are designed for high-volume use by fleets. They are an attractive option for a trucking firm, since they avoid the percentage up-charges of credit card companies, while also saving on the price of fuel. With a fuel card, prices are set at the wholesale level, rather than the standard (and higher) retail price. All purchases made using a fuel card are consolidated onto a single weekly invoice, which is payable by direct debit from the company's bank account. Switching to a single weekly invoice from the many receipts associated with individual fuel purchases also reduces the accounting work associated with recording fuel purchases.

---

[3] A load board is a freight matching service that helps to connect shippers and carriers.

Use Cash Back Credit Cards

A useful cost control is to obtain a company credit card that pays back a percentage of all purchases made on it, and then try to make the bulk of your purchases with this card. Several cards offer cash-back rates of two percent, which can bolster your profits to a significant extent.

Tip: The rules for what constitutes a cash back offer and what does not varies by credit card, and sometimes even for the same card over time. Also, cashback amounts may be capped. Consequently, it may make sense to conduct an annual review of available credit card deals, and switch to whichever one makes the most sense for your business.

Require Meal Receipt Storage

Meals purchased while on the road are tax deductible, so it makes sense to have a fool-proof way to store these receipts during jobs. One approach is to supply a brightly-colored receipts envelope to each driver, to be stored in their truck. All meal receipts are to be stored in it during a job, and turned in to the bookkeeper once the job is over, to be replaced by a new envelope. This involves training not just the drivers in why it is important to collect meal receipts, but also the bookkeeper, who should request the envelope at the end of every job. If the envelope is not handed over, then you will probably need to have a word with the driver about why these receipts are so important. They need to understand that losing a meal receipt increases the income taxes that the company will have to pay.

Record No-Receipt Payments

As was the case with meals, any other business payments made while on the road are tax-deductible, and of course the receipts should be saved for all of them. But what about cases in which no receipt is provided by the seller? This is most commonly an issue when payments are made with bills or coins. When this is the case, have drivers record the expenditures in a log, which can then be used as evidence of payment.

Tip: Prepare a formal receipts log for your drivers, in which they record the amount paid, where the payment was made, the date of payment, and the reason why it was made. Also, have them initial each expenditure line item.

Reconcile the Bank Statement

Reconciling the bank statement means checking to see if your internal records of cash receipts and expenditures match those in the bank's records for your checking account. This is extremely worthwhile, for several reasons. First, it is quite likely that you will make a mistake when recording a few accounting transactions in your books, which you will spot during the reconciliation. Second, the bank charges a variety of fees, such as for account maintenance, wire transfers, ordering additional check stock, cashing not sufficient funds checks, and so forth. By conducting a reconciliation, you can spot these items and record them in the company's books; doing so adjusts your cash balance to what is actually on hand. And finally, it is possible (though rare) that the bank will make a mistake in how it records your transactions. If so, a reconciliation is the only way you will spot these items, and then make the bank aware of them.

> **Tip:** If you have time, access the bank's records online every day, so that you can conduct a daily reconciliation. Doing so is a good way to spot errors as soon as they occur.

Maintain Warranty Records

Much of the equipment operated by a trucking firm has a warranty associated with it, which can save you large amounts in the event of an unexpected equipment failure. To ensure that you have the paperwork associated with every warranty, store it in a clearly-identified folder in a fireproof safe. In addition, summarize the warranty information on a spreadsheet, so that you can easily review the warranty situation for all key assets held by the business.

Conduct Maintenance on Schedule

Always conduct scheduled maintenance on your trucks. Doing so minimizes the risk of break-downs during jobs, which imperil delivery times and could injure your drivers. Avoiding unplanned breakdowns also minimizes the higher cost of dealing with towing charges and having to pay more extensive repair bills. In short, the lower and more frequent cost of scheduled maintenance is much cheaper in the long run than the higher cost of unplanned breakdowns.

> **Tip:** Maintain a separate maintenance record for each truck, covering oil changes, tires, brakes and engine rebuilds. This is useful for slotting future maintenance activity in-between jobs.

Establish a Freight Lane

A *freight lane* is any route that your firm covers on a regular schedule. These lanes may connect a number of cities or transport hubs. They might be direct point-to-point routes, or connect multiple points, and travel in any direction. They might take a few days to travel, or span a period of months. By operating with an established freight lane, a trucking firm can standardize its monthly revenue, transporting loads for the same set of customers along the lane. Customers appreciate the consistent availability of your trucks, and so are more likely to send more business your way. This approach also concentrates your attention on procuring more loads along the lane, so that deadhead miles are minimized (see next).

Freight lanes should be established where there are lots of cargos, minimal toll booths, relatively frequent maintenance facilities, and travel across generally flat terrain. These factors make it easier to boost your revenue, minimize costs and deal with repairs as expeditiously as possible.

Avoid Deadhead Miles

Deadhead miles are the miles driven with an empty load, either returning home or driving to a new destination to pick up a new load. The concept differs slightly from *bobtailing*, which is when you're driving a cargo truck with no semi-trailer hooked up. In either case, the miles driven are not profitable, since there is no load to carry. From a safety perspective, it is especially important to avoid deadhead miles. Trailers have a massive sail area, and can be flipped by high wind when they are not loaded with cargo.

It is nearly impossible to completely avoid deadhead miles, but there are some ways to reduce them. They are as follows:

- *Get paid for it.* Search for jobs where the shipper or broker is willing to pay a certain amount per deadhead mile driven. While the amount paid will likely not generate a profit, it can significantly reduce your costs.
- *Look for return loads.* Search for jobs that require loads for the return trip. Some brokers can be accommodating in setting up return loads, but you may have to check with nearby shippers or brokers for the business.
- *Check load boards.* Search online load boards for available freight on your targeted route.

Enhance Driver and Truck Efficiency

A good way to reduce fuel costs is to improve the efficiency of both the driver and the truck. Here are several options to pursue:

- Add a roof fairing and trailer side skirts to improve aerodynamics
- Avoid rapid accelerations and decelerations
- Drive at a somewhat lower speed
- Install low-rolling-resistance tires
- Install lower-weight aluminum wheels
- Maintain the correct tire pressure
- Minimize off-route driving
- Reduce the amount of idling time
- Use larger dual fuel tanks to minimize refueling stops[4]

---

[4] A dual-tank system also allows drivers to stock up on the least-expensive fuel whenever they find it.

Enforce Cargo Protection Policies

A lost cargo can result in substantial losses, so enforce a common-sense set of policies that are targeted at cargo protection. This means requiring drivers to manually check all truck locks before leaving the truck for any break periods. Another policy should mandate that a standard checklist be followed to ensure that the cargo has been properly secured before starting up a truck. Any violation of these policies should be taken extremely seriously, including termination of a driver's employment with the company.

Properly Store Logbooks

Driver logbooks contain information about the hours that a driver spends driving, as well as their off-duty hours. While this might not seem like an accounting issue, logbooks can provide valuable information about what drivers were doing during the times when the company is claiming tax-deductible expenses, such as meal costs. Consequently, if only for their value as evidence, driver logbooks should be carefully stored. Consider storing them in a fireproof safe, as already recommended for warranty records.

Note: If an electronic logging device (ELD) is used instead of a logbook, verify that the information collected in this manner is properly backed up and readily accessible.

Reduce Insurance Costs

An insurer will charge somewhat less for your liability insurance when you have built up a long-term record of above-average driver safety and minimal accidents. This places an emphasis on prudent hiring, to bring in drivers with lots of experience and few accidents on their driving records. Insurance premiums can also be reduced by avoiding certain types of cargos, such as hazardous chemicals. Another possibility is to use smaller and older trucks, for which insurance premiums are typically lower. However, you may find that the prices garnered from the transport of hazardous chemicals offset their increased insurance cost, and you may also prefer to run newer trucks on the grounds that they require less maintenance. In short, you may choose to ignore some of the factors that can drive down insurance costs.

Summary

Proper cost control is an absolutely essential ingredient of success in the trucking industry. This is not an area in which you can passively operate a business and watch the profits roll in. On the contrary, trucking firms are subject to the vagaries of bad weather, spikes in fuel prices, seasonal demand, and deadheading miles – all of which can eat into profits. In short, an obsessive focus on cost reductions is one of the best ways to ensure that your business prospers.

Chapter 7
Trucker Metrics

Introduction

Given the low margins that most trucking businesses earn, it makes sense to closely monitor every aspect of them. In this chapter, we cover several metrics that require the input of a certain amount of accounting information. Additional operational metrics will likely be needed in order to maintain tight control over every possible aspect of the business.

Revenue per Mile

The first step in determining a firm's profit per mile is to calculate its revenue per mile. This should be relatively easy to determine. Simply add up your monthly billed revenue and divide by the number of miles driven during the month. Thus, if revenues are $50,000 and the miles driven were 27,500, then the revenue per mile would be $1.82.

Cost per Mile

An essential measurement for any trucking operation is a determination of how much it is costing you per mile. It is quite useful for setting the baseline revenue level below which you cannot afford to accept jobs. For example, one approach is to write down the odometer reading at the beginning and end of each month and divide the resulting miles for the period into your operating cost for that truck – which should include driver pay and benefits, fuel, tolls, maintenance and repairs, insurance, tires, permits, and licenses. For example, if costs are $42,625 and the miles driven were 27,500, then the cost per mile would be $1.55.

Profit per Mile

The ultimate measure of trucker profitability is profit per mile. It is derived by subtracting the cost per mile from the revenue per mile. To continue with the preceding examples, this would mean that revenue per mile of $1.82 minus a cost per mile of $1.55 would result in a profit per mile of $0.27, which is roughly 15% of the revenue figure.

Fuel Cost per Gallon

It can be useful to divide the cost of fuel by the number of gallons purchased. From a management perspective, this is most useful when tracked at a finer level of detail, such as by state, freight lane, or individual truck. This information can be used to conduct searches for less-expensive fuel, or to adjust routes to take advantage of lower fuel costs.

Days Sales Outstanding

When evaluating the amount of accounts receivable outstanding, it is best to compare the receivables to the sales activity of the business, in order to see the proportion of receivables to sales. This proportion can be expressed as the average number of days over which receivables are outstanding before they are paid, which is called days sales outstanding, or DSO. DSO is the most popular of all collection measurements.

Days sales outstanding is most useful when compared to the standard number of days that customers are allowed before payment is due. Thus, a DSO figure of 40 days might initially appear excellent, until you realize that the standard payment terms are only 15 days. A combination of prudent credit granting and robust collections activity is the likely cause when the DSO figure is only a few days longer than the standard payment terms. From a management perspective, it is easiest to spot collection problems at a gross level by tracking DSO on a trend line, and watching for a sudden spike in the measurement in comparison to what was reported in prior periods.

To calculate DSO, divide 365 days into the amount of annual credit sales to arrive at credit sales per day, and then divide this figure into the average accounts receivable for the measurement period. Thus, the formula is:

$$\frac{\text{Average accounts receivable}}{\text{Annual sales} \div 365 \text{ days}}$$

EXAMPLE

The bookkeeper of MacPherson Trucking wants to derive the days sales outstanding for the company for the April reporting period. In April, the beginning and ending accounts receivable balances were $420,000 and $540,000, respectively. The total credit sales for the 12 months ended April 30 were $4,000,000. The bookkeeper derives the following DSO calculation from this information:

$$\frac{(\$420,000 \text{ Beginning receivables} + \$540,000 \text{ Ending receivables}) \div 2}{\$4,000,000 \text{ Credit sales} \div 365 \text{ Days}}$$

$$=$$

$$\frac{\$480,000 \text{ Average accounts receivable}}{\$10,959 \text{ Credit sales per day}}$$

$$= 43.8 \text{ Days}$$

Days Payables Outstanding

The accounts payable days formula measures the number of days that a company takes to pay its suppliers. If the number of days increases from one period to the next, this indicates that the company is paying its suppliers more slowly. A change in the number of payable days can also indicate altered payment terms with suppliers, though this rarely has more than a slight impact on the total number of days. If a company is paying its suppliers very quickly, it may mean that the suppliers are demanding short payment terms because they are suspicious of the company's ability to pay.

To calculate days payables outstanding, summarize all purchases from suppliers during the measurement period, and divide by the average amount of accounts payable during that period. The formula is:

$$\frac{\text{Total supplier purchases}}{(\text{Beginning accounts payable} + \text{Ending accounts payable}) \div 2}$$

This formula reveals the total accounts payable turnover. Then divide the resulting turnover figure into 365 days to arrive at the number of accounts payable days.

The formula can be modified to exclude cash payments to suppliers, since the numerator should include only purchases on credit from suppliers. However, the amount of up-front cash payments to suppliers is normally so small that this modification is not necessary.

As an example, a bookkeeper wants to determine his company's accounts payable days for the past year. In the beginning of this period, the beginning accounts payable balance was $800,000, and the ending balance was $884,000. Purchases for the last 12 months were $7,500,000. Based on this information, the bookkeeper calculates the accounts payable turnover as:

$$\frac{\$7,500,000 \text{ Purchases}}{(\$800,000 \text{ Beginning payables} + \$884,000 \text{ Ending payables}) \div 2}$$

$$=$$

$$\frac{\$7,500,000 \text{ Purchases}}{\$842,000 \text{ Average accounts payable}}$$

$$= 8.9 \text{ Accounts payable turnover}$$

Thus, the company's accounts payable is turning over at a rate of 8.9 times per year. To calculate the turnover in days, the bookkeeper divides the 8.9 turns into 365 days, which yields:

$$365 \text{ Days} \div 8.9 \text{ Turns} = 41 \text{ Days}$$

A significant failing of the days payables outstanding measurement is that it does not factor in all of the short-term liabilities of a business. There may be substantial liabilities related to payroll, interest, and taxes that exceed the size of payables out-standing. This issue can be eliminated by incorporating all short-term liabilities into the measurement.

Summary

The ratios in this chapter were largely derived from accounting data. Other metrics that only use operational metrics may also be of use, such as truck downtime, average truck speed, engine runtime, equipment utilization, transit time, proportion of loaded miles, on-time delivery, preventive maintenance compliance, driver turnover, and time-per-drop.

Glossary

A

Account. A separate, detailed record about a specific item, such as expenditures for office supplies, or accounts receivable, or accounts payable.

Accounting cycle. A sequential set of activities used to identify and record an entity's individual transactions.

Accounting equation. The concept that assets equal the sum of all liabilities and shareholders' equity.

Accounting transaction. A business event having a monetary impact on the financial statements of a business.

Accrual. A journal entry that is used to recognize revenues and expenses that have been earned or consumed, respectively, and for which the related source documents have not yet been received or generated.

Accrual basis of accounting. The concept of recording revenues when earned and expenses as incurred.

B

Balance sheet. A report that lists the assets, liabilities, and equity of the business as of the report date.

Bobtailing. When you're driving a cargo truck with no semi-trailer hooked up.

Breakeven point. The sales volume at which a business earns exactly no money, where all contribution margin earned is needed to pay for the firm's fixed costs.

C

Cash basis of accounting. The practice of only recording revenue when cash is received from a customer, and recording expenses only when cash has been paid out.

Cash equivalent. A short-term, very liquid investment that is easily convertible into a known amount of cash, and which is so near its maturity that it presents an insignificant risk of a change in value because of changes in interest rates.

Claims-made policy. An insurance policy that only provides coverage for claims made during a specific date range.

Contribution margin. A service's price minus all variable costs, resulting in the incremental profit earned for each unit of service provided.

D

Deadhead miles. The miles driven with an empty load.

Depreciation. The planned, gradual reduction in the recorded value of an asset over its useful life by charging it to expense.

Double entry accounting. A record keeping system under which every transaction is recorded in at least two accounts.

F

Factoring. When a lender buys your company's accounts receivable at a discount.

Filing segment. The name under which a record is both stored and later requested by users.

Financial accounting. The recordation of information about money.

Fixed cost. A cost that does not increase or decrease in conjunction with any activities.

Follower block. A metal plate at the back of a file drawer that can be adjusted to reduce the effective length of the drawer.

Freight lane. Any route that a trucking firm covers on a regular schedule.

G

General folder. A folder containing records that involve small volumes, where there is no need for a specially-designated folder.

General ledger. The master set of all accounts, in which are stored all of the business transactions that have been entered into the accounts with journal entries or software module entries.

Guide. A rigid cardboard or plastic divider that is used to signal the start of a new section within a group of records.

I

Income statement. A report that lists the revenues, expenses, and profit or loss of the business for a specific period of time.

Individual folder. A folder used to store only the records for a specific correspondent; it is typically employed when there is a sufficient volume of records to warrant a separate folder.

J

Journal entry. A formalized method for recording a business transaction.

L

Load board. A freight matching service that helps to connect shippers and carriers.

O

Occurrence policy. An insurance policy that provides coverage for events occurring within a specific date range.

OUT indicator. A sheet or folder that indicates the location of records that have been removed from storage.

P

Payroll register. The primary internal report generated by the payroll system. It itemizes the calculation of wages, taxes, and deductions for each employee for each payroll.

Personal property. Assets that are movable, and so may include furniture and fixtures, vehicles, and collectibles.

R

Real property. Any property that is directly attached to the land, plus land itself.

Realization principle. The concept that revenue can only be recognized once the underlying goods or services associated with the revenue have been delivered or rendered, respectively.

Record. Stored information used as evidence and information, and which has value by being retained for a certain period of time.

S

Score mark. Indented lines along the bottom edge of a folder that can be folded to expand the storage capacity of the folder.

Source documents. The physical basis upon which business transactions are recorded.

Special guide. The same as a guide, which indicates sub-levels of information within a record storage location.

Statement of cash flows. A report that lists the cash inflows and outflows generated by the business for a specific period of time.

T

Transaction. A business event that has a monetary impact.

Trial balance. An itemization of the debit and credit totals for each account.

Index